LONSDALE

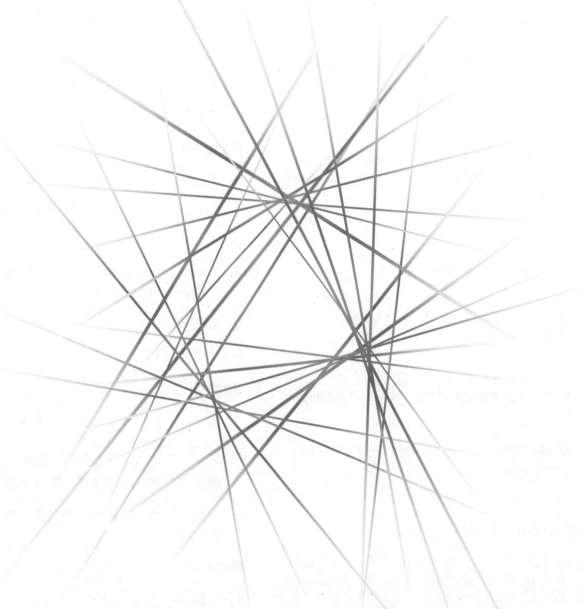

ESSENTIALS

GCSE Design & Technology
Food Technology
Workbook Answers

Page 4

1. C

2. **a)** low, **b)** are, **c)** 3 tbsp, **d)** should.

3. A, C, D

4. healthy, eating, fat, saturated, sugar, increasing.

5. A2, B3, C1

Page 5

1. balancing, physical, maintain, more, needs, overweight, controlled, increases, seriously, obese.

2. To tackle rising rates of obesity.

3. A, C, D, E, G

4. Lower obesity and excess weight.

5. B

Page 6

1. C, E, F

2. So they can make informed choices about buying food.

3. **a)** less, **b)** high blood pressure, **c)** less, **d)** 5g, **e)** dental caries.

4. C

5. The addition of nutrients to food.

Page 7

1. B, D

2. By using a computer program.

3. calories, all, brain activity, asleep, active, energy, food.

4. A4, B3, C1, D2

Page 8

1. A, B, C

2. amino acids, protein, thousands, absorbed, eleven, diet, essential

3. A, B, D, E, G, H

4. A, C, D, F, G

5. To ensure your body receives all the essential amino acids.

Page 9

1. cheaper, less, easy, more.

2. A3, B1, C2

3. **a)** versatile, **b)** bland, **c)** manufacture, **d)** meat.

4. A, C, D

Page 10

1. **a)** provide, **b)** protect, **c)** warm, **d)** soluble.

2. Fats are solid at room temperature, oils are liquid.

3. B, C, E, F, H

4. Because it raises the cholesterol level. This can lead to heart and health problems.

5. A, C, H

6. Hydrogen

Page 11

1. eliminate, fibre, cholesterol, energy.

2. A3, B1, C2

3. **a)** instant, **b)** sugars, **c)** fat, **d)** obesity, **e)** tooth decay.

4. Because the energy is released more slowly during the race.

Page 12

1. A, B, D

2. **a)** some, **b)** daily, **c)** wide, **d)** shouldn't, **e)** fat.

3. B

4. **a)** spina bifida, **b)** eyes, **c)** water, **d)** B complex, **e)** poisonous, **f)** sunlight, **g)** vitamin C, **h)** orange.

Page 13

1. A, C, D

2. A4, B3, C5, D1, E2

3. C, D, F

4. 2–3 litres.

5. essential, dehydrated, lubricated, constipation, control, death, urine, fatal.

Page 14

1. choices, factors, dietary, ethical.

2. So that she and the baby are healthy.

3. A, C, E, H

4. **a)** Raw, **b)** Excess, **c)** liver, **d)** miscarriage, **e)** sword fish, **f)** Unpasteurised.

5. A, B, D

Page 15

1. A, D, F, G

2. **a)** insulin, **b)** two, **c)** injections, **d)** maturity, **e)** diet, **f)** exercise, **g)** healthy.

3. **a)** common, **b)** lactase, **c)** sugar, **d)** Soya, **e)** enzyme.

4. Soya milk.

Page 16

1. allergies, immune, serious, intolerances.

2. D

3. **a)** small, **b)** severe, **c)** airways, **d)** lowered, **e)** death, **f)** adrenaline.

4. A sensitivity to gluten, which is a protein found in wheat.

5. A, C, E

Page 17

1. A3, B4, C2, D1

2. Meat which has been slaughtered in a special way.

3. avoid, meat, religious, environment, health.

4. B, D, E

5. Because prawns are caught by trawlers producing greenhouse gases, then transported across the world to be peeled, deep frozen and shipped back.

Page 18

1. A, B, D, F, G, H

2. Vegans don't eat any food from animal origins. Vegetarians don't eat products obtained by killing animals but may eat products such as eggs and milk.

3. C

4. **a)** without, **b)** don't, **c)** expanding, **d)** inconclusive, **e)** ethical.

5. **a)** soil, **b)** energy, **c)** greenhouse, **d)** wildlife, **e)** lower.

Page 19

1. A, E, F, G

2. Inspectors trained by Assured Food Standards (AFS), which is a not-for-profit organisation.

3. independent, guarantees, farmers, economically, fair.

4. A, C, D

5. **a)** altered, **b)** aren't, **c)** less, **d)** resistant, **e)** more.

Page 20

1. problems, national, planning, solve.

2. Food miles refers to the distance food travels from where it is produced to where it is eaten.

3. A, B, C, E

4. People in poor countries rely on selling us their crops. If we don't buy them they will suffer financial hardship.

5. Carbon dioxide.

6. **a)** less, **b)** minimal, **c)** energy, **d)** reduces, **e)** methane.

Page 21

1. **a)** remove, **b)** CO_2, **c)** global, **d)** palm, **e)** biscuits, **f)** animals.

2. Global warming is caused by CO_2 emissions trapping the Sun's energy.

3. cows, methane, twenty, harmful, GHG, entire, chicken, lamb.

4. B

Page 22

1. **a)** carcass, **b)** liver, **c)** poultry, **d)** meat.

2. A, C, D

3. A3, B4, C2, D1

4. **a)–b) any two from:** It changes colour, connective

tissue becomes gelatine, extractions released, non-enzymic browning takes place.

5. **a)** bottom, **b)** sealed, **c)** separate, **d)** cooked, **e)** immediately.

Page 23

1. **a)–c) in any order:** White fish, oily fish, shell fish.

2. A, C, D.

3. A4, B5, C2, D3, E1.

4. **a)** high, **b)** covered, **c)** sea, **d)** without, **e)** canned, **f)** poached.

5. D

Page 24

1. cows, homogenised, pressure, globules, deteriorates, shelf, bacteria.

2. A4, B1, C2, D5, E3.

3. **a)** two, **b)** water, **c)** sterilised.

4. B

Page 25

1. A, B, C, E, G

2. **a)** dairy, **b)** churning, **c)** margarine, **d)** fat, **e)** bacterial, **f)** solid.

3. D

4. third, fat, separates, coagulate, digest.

5. Dairy foods should be stored in the fridge, except for dried, condensed, sterilised and evaporated milk.

Page 26

1. A, B, D, E,

2. A4, B6, C1, D5, E2, F3

3. Fruit and vegetables can be preserved at home by freezing, pickling, and jamming.

4. **a)** prepared, **b)** raw, **c)** liquid, **d)** lid.

Page 27

1. B

2. Manufacturers use liquid, frozen or spray dried Class B eggs.

3. **a)** code, **b)** barn, **c)** blunt, **d)** smelling.

4. Egg whites coagulate at 60°C.

5. **a)** meringues, **b)** emulsify, **c)** hold ingredients together, **d)** thicken.

Page 28

1. A, C, E, F, G

2. **a)** solid, **b)** liquid, **c)** fridge, **d)** room, **e)** solidify, **f)** needed, **g)** obese.

3. B, D, E

4. Because fat is high in calories and can cause you to become overweight or obese.

5. **a)** Butter, **b)** short, **c)** creamed, **d)** extend shelf life, **e)** colour.

Page 29

1. **a)–b) In any order:** Sugar beet, sugar cane.

2. D

3. sticky, bacteria, teeth, break, acid, enamel, decay.

4. **a)** low, **b)** similar, **c)** smaller, **d)** over, **e)** dextrinisation.

5. A, C, D, E, G

Page 30

1. So designers can make sure the new dishes match the product profile.

2. A, B, C

3. liquid, solid, separate, stand.

4. **a)** solid, **b)** don't, **c)** agitated, **d)** suspension.

5. solid, liquid, gelling.

6. B, C, D

Page 31

1. Smart starches have been altered to change their working properties.

2. B

3. mix, immiscible, unstable, separates, stable, emulsifier, lecithin.

4. A, C

5. a) gas, b) light, c) Meringue.

6. C

Page 32

1. Gluten is formed when water is added to glutenin and gliadin in wheat.

2. B

3. A, C

4. cakes, crumbly, coating, starch, flour, liquid, gluten.

5. a) short, b) long, c) crumbly, d) starch.

Page 33

1. a) bacteria, b) sour, c) curd, d) cheese.

2. C

3. A3, B1, C2

4. A

5. raising, bicarbonate, heat, carbonate, steam, dioxide.

6. To make the centre chewy.

Page 34

1. a) gas, b) expand, c) rise, d) mechanical.

2. D

3. A3, B1, C2

4. B, D

5. An open, uneven texture.

Page 35

1. a)–d) in any order: warmth, liquid, food, time.

2. D

3. They produce carbon dioxide when heated with a liquid.

4. alkali, carbon dioxide, heated, yellow, soapy, strong, gingerbread.

5. A, B, D, F

Page 36

1. a) digest, b) bulky, c) preserve, d) palatability, e) texture.

2. It is changed physically and chemically.

3. A3, B4, C2, D1

4. converted, magnetron, travel, molecules, friction, heat.

Page 37

1. A2, B4, C1, D3

2. a) wholemeal, b) surface, c) enrobing, d) fruit.

3. a) colour, b) dextrinisation, c) air, d) moisture, e) softens, f) structure.

4. Aeration means trapping air in the mixture.

5. B

Page 38

1. a) binds, b) dextrinisation, c) shorten, d) steam.

2. A, C, D, E

3. A2, B3, C4, D1.

4. B

Page 39

1. Strong plain flour.

2. C

3. a) gluten, b) salt, c) carbon, d) framework.

4. size, flour, wholemeal, appearance, toppings, poppy.

5. A2, B3, C1.

Page 40

1. Liquids that are thickened.

2. flavour, sweet, moist, nutritive, bind.

3. Manufacturers use modified starches to prevent synerisis occurring. This happens when proteins are overcooked. They continue to coagulate, squeezing out the fat and water which is seen as a thin liquid that has separated from the sauce.

4. a) sink, b) break open, c) gelatinisation, d) gel, e) solidify.

5. The nutritional value would be altered. The sauce would contain fewer calories and would be useful if you were following a reduced fat diet.

Page 41

1. Changing the recipe to produce an amended product.

2. D

3. A, B, C, E, G

4. **a)** Quorn, **b)** cheese, **c)** circles, **d)** processor, **e)** dressing, **f)** scone.

5. **a)–b) Any two of:** trifle, moussaka, tiramisu or any other sensible answer.

6. **a)–c) in any order:** crumble, pastry (any type), sponge mixture, or any sensible answer

Page 42

1. change, time, harmful, hanging, tender, blue, moulds, unpleasant.

2. B

3. cells, animal, ripen.

4. A3, B1, C2

Page 43

1. Yeasts are single celled organisms found in the air and on skins of fruit.

2. A, B, C, D

3. B, C

4. **a)** air, **b)** acidic, **c)** moist, **d)** are destroyed by.

5. fresh, badly, moulds, allergic, problems, poisonous substances.

6. B, D

Page 44

1. Bacteria are single-celled organisms which are able to reproduce rapidly.

2. A, C, D, E, G

3. cooked, high, contaminated, destroyed, eaten.

4. A, C, D, E

5. **a)** separate, **b)** different, **c)** cooked, **d)** safe.

Page 45

1. A, C, D

2. They may get Listeria Monocytogenes which can cause miscarriage or premature births.

3. D

4. Because Staphylococcus Aureus lives in the nasal passages and throats of humans and is found in human excretia.

5. B, D, F

6. Most food poisoning happens because the consumer doesn't follow storage and reheating instructions given by the manufacturer.

Page 46

1. B, D, F, G, H

2. The danger zone is the temperature between 3°C and 63°C at which bacteria can reproduce rapidly.

3. A4, B1, C5, D3, E2

4. **a)** moist, **b)** remove, **c)** drying, **d)** sugar, **e)** salt, **f)** solid.

Page 47

1. rapidly, million, seven, control, quickly, cooked, cooled, fridge.

2. Bacteria can't survive below pH3.5. Vinegar has a pH of 4.5 so it prevents bacteria growing.

3. A, B, C

4. A, C, D

5. **a)** won't, **b)** must.

Page 48

1. HACCP – Hazard Analysis Critical Control Point.

2. A, C, D, F, G

3. **a)** hot, **b)** immediately, **c)** antibacterial, **d)** steam, **e)** rapidly, **f)** probe.

4. A2, B6, C5, D1, E3, F4

Page 49

1. Shelf life is the time food is safe to eat or is in the best condition.

2. sell, unsafe, enjoy, preservation, extend.

3. B

4. C

5. **a)** prevents, **b)** delays, **c)** preserves, **d)** removal, **e)** high.

Page 50

1. At low temperatures bacteria become dormant (don't reproduce but aren't dead).

2. B, C, D

3. D

4. **a)** cream, short, **b)** ready, cooled, 90, five.

5. D

6. Quick freezing creates small ice crystals that do less damage to the cells.

Page 51

1. **a)** checked, **b)** defrosted, **c)** sensors, **d)** shut, **e)** recorded.

2. They may be requested by environmental health officers.

3. D

4. B

5. **a)** freezing, **b)** vacuum, **c)** vapour, **d)** light.

Page 52

1. **a)** short, 15, shelf, some, **b)** (UHT), time, 130°C, months.

2. D

3. Because of the caramelisation of the lactose (milk sugar).

4. **a)** sterilisation, **b)** sterilised, **c)** re-contamination, **d)** long.

5. A, C, E

Page 53

1. A3, B1, C2

2. The E number indicates the additive has passed the European Community Safety Standards. The E number code is used in place of complicated chemical names.

3. C, F, G

4. **a)** set, **b)** stronger, **c)** enzymic browning, **d)** calories, **e)** separating.

5. E.

Page 54

1. food, invention, longer, re-invented, keep.

2. A, B, C, D, G

3. **a)** can, increased, **b)** luxury, **c)** Some, **d)** reduced, **e)** increasing.

4. B, D E

Page 55

1. target, specification, factors, research, launched.

2. **a)** brief, **b)** design, **c)** designer, factors.

3. B and C

4. B

Page 56

1. A 2, B 3, C 1

2. A and C

3. guideline, initial, intended.

4. **a)** manufacturer, **b)** write down, **c)** consumer, **d)** before.

Page 57

1. A, C, D

2. **a)** photograph, **b)** packaging, **c)** tolerances, **d)** storage.

3. A, B, D, E, F, H

Page 58

1. identical, shape, problem, specific.

2. C

3. A, B, D

4. C, D

5. time, supply, sensory, companies, components.

Page 59

1. **a)** primary, original, didn't, **b)** secondary, information, collected, someone.

2. A, C, D, G

3. Disassembly means taking things apart.

4. B, C, H

Page 60

1. **a)** find, **b)** Spreadsheets, **c)** speed up, **d)** database, **e)** video conferencing.

2. A, B, D

3. B

4. till, database, selling.

Page 61

1. Modelling is the representation of a real object on the computer screen.

2. **a)** bacteria, **b)** structure, **c)** manufacture, **d)** ingredients, **e)** costs.

3. make, predict, recipe.

4. B, D, E

Page 62

1. prototypes, test, money.

2. **a)** consistent, **b)** outcome, **c)** avoided.

3. A, B, D, E, F.

4. industry, HACCP, train, operate, safely.

5. Use the correct knife for the task, hold by the handle, keep fingers away from blade, use a bridge or claw for slicing. Cut on a stable surface. Don't have greasy hands.

Page 63

1. **a)** schools, **b)** the same, **c)** Electric.

2. CIM is used in large scale food manufacture where the entire process is controlled by computers.

3. A8, B7, C4, D3, E6, F5, G1, H2.

4. A, C, D

Page 64

1. analysis, senses, like, five, eat, food.

2. A, B, D, F, G

3. D

4. **a)** controlled, **b)** can be changed, **c)** small, **d)** identical, **e)** code.

5. A, B, D

Page 65

1. B

2. evaluating, trained, sensory, private.

3. A, D

4. D

Page 66

1. D

2. **a)** two, **b)** triangle, **c)** three, **d)** A not A.

3. **a)** triangle, same, different, identify, **b)** control, two, like, identify.

4. A, B, D

Page 67

1. Diagrams showing complex systems.

2. B

3. A2, B3, C1

4. systems, BSI, make, manufacturer, production, quality.

Page 68

1. **a)** scale, predicted, shelf, **b)** time, delivered, waste.

2. D

3. A, D

4. **a)** Batch production, **b)** skilled, **c)** can,
d) Continuous flow, **e)** unskilled.

Page 69

1. Computer Aided Manufacture.

2. A, C, D, F, G

3. **a)** load cell, **b)** light detector, **c)** micro-biological,
d) light refractor, **e)** metal.

4. control, remedial, automatic, computer, alarm, blown,
pushed, production.

Page 70

1. B

2. safe, taste, reliable, buy.

3. ISO9000 certificate.

4. **a)** consumers', **b)** health, **c)** reliable, **d)** Maintenance,
e) Safe, **f)** records, **g)** Safe, **h)** relations.

Page 71

1. A, C, D

2. The manufacturer will be investigated by
Environmental Health officers. The business could
be closed. The manufacturer could be fined or sent
to prison.

3. A, B, D

4. A, C, D, F, G

5. The safety of food is checked to make sure that it
doesn't cause illness when you eat it.

Page 72

1. Hazard Analysis Critical Control Point.

2. analysis, wrong, stop, food, HACCP.

3. A3, B1, C2

4. **a)** harvesting, **b)** manufacturer, **c)** transportation,
d) storage, **e)** reheating.

Page 73

1. **a)** processes, **b)** risks, **c)** critical, **d)** removed,
e) tolerances, **f)** monitored, **g)** problem.

2. C

3. First In First Out – used in stock rotation to make
sure the oldest product is used first.

4. Basic Food Hygiene Certificate.

5. B

Page 74

1. The European Union (EU).

2. legal, law, language, understood, inform, accurate.

3. B

4. A, B, D, E, G, H

Page 75

1. farm, clear, market, suitable.

2. C

3. A, B, C, E, F

4. A3, B1, C2

Page 76

1. A3, B1, C2

2. **a)** extends, **b)** transportation, **c)** advertise,
d) physical, **e)** tampering.

3. A, B, D

4. transparent, heat, recycled, breakable, transport.

Page 77

1. C

2. It reacts with some foods so some cans must be
lined.

3. **a)** individual, **b)** Some, **c)** advantage, **d)** cheap,
e) easy.

4. A, B, D

5. D

Page 78

1. **a)** ii, **b)** iv **c)** iii, **d)** ii, **e)** i, **f)** iv, **g)** ii, **h)** iv

Page 79

1. **i)** iii, **j)** iii, **k)** iv, **l)** ii, **m)** iii, **n)** iii, **o)** iii

1. **A good high scoring answer would include the following information:**

   - They may use nutritional labelling – so consumers are aware of the nutritional value of the product and can make an informed choice. This may show the percentage of RDA. Or they may use a traffic light system – this isn't a legal requirement. The use of different systems can confuse consumers (you could explain this in detail; red, amber and green).
   - Reduced the amount of sugar, fat (especially saturated fat) and salt in processed food because of the detrimental effect on health e.g. coronary heart disease, some cancers, type 2 diabetes, high blood pressure, osteoarthritis, and tooth decay.
   - Modified existing dishes to meet healthy guidelines by using alternative ingredients or cooking methods, e.g. replace beef with Quorn, grill instead of bake.
   - Targeted specific groups when marketing eg healthy snacks for children.
   - Used organic foods which some consumers prefer because they are produced without the use of chemical pesticides, fungicides or synthetic drugs. The benefits of the nutritional value of organic foods are not yet proven.

2. **a)** **To make sure you have answered this question both ideas should be *different*. For both ideas make sure that you have included the following:**
   - A sketch of the product, 2D/3D or cross section or a combination of these labelled to show...
     - Bread base
     - Savoury filling or topping
     - Organic vegetables
     - Any other ingredients used.
   - Some indication of the portion size.
   - That the product can be eaten hot or cold and the cooking or reheating method.

   You might also include in the answer:
   - Suitability for mass production.
   - Nutritional information.
   - Details of texture, flavour, colour, shape, dimensions.
   - Storage details.
   - Suitability for special dietary needs giving examples such as vegetarian.

2. **b)** You should have chosen one of the ideas outlined in 2. a).

2. **c)**

Criteria	How it is met
Use a bread base	Made from strong plain flour or wholemeal flour and yeast. Or named ready made standard component e.g. deep pan pizza base or thin and crispy pizza base.
Have a savoury filling /topping	Name the ingredients e.g. passata, named cheese.
Contain organic vegetables	Name the vegetables.
Be able to be eaten hot or cold	Details of storage e.g. chilling cabinet, fridge. Reheating instructions e.g. microwave or oven.

2. **d)** **When answering this question you should remember that the product is to be made in a *test kitchen* so you should not include any large scale production methods or packaging.**

   Your idea must be logical and clear to gain high marks.

   You should indicate any preparation which is necessary, e.g.:
   - Kitchen and personal hygiene, giving examples.
   - Any preparation of ingredients, e.g. weighing and washing.
   - Any equipment required, e.g. a preheated oven.

   You should show exactly **how** the product is made (base and topping).
   - Use the correct terms, e.g. kneading, mixing, chopping etc...
   - Some time management could be indicated, e.g. dove-tailing of tasks, while the dough is rising prepare the topping.

   Control checks should be shown and should include some reference to:
   - Temperature, e.g. oven, water, cooling before storage.
   - Time, e.g. cooking time, leaving bread base to rise.

- Portion control and an explanation of exactly how this will be done, e.g. weighing and measuring.
- Checks on size and shape, giving details and dimensions.
- Food safety, giving any examples of personal and equipment hygiene.
- Safety precautions through safe use of equipment.

Page 84

2. e)

Ingredient for Pizza Base	Reason for use
Strong plain flour	Bulk ingredient Forms structure Contains gluten for elasticity
Sugar	Food for yeast Flavour
Salt	Flavour enhancer
Yeast	Gives off CO_2 raising agent
Water	Binds ingredients Adds moisture and warmth Develops gluten

3. a) Plain flour or plain wholemeal flour.

Page 85

3. b) In the rubbing in method, fat is 'rubbed in' to flour. Plasticity allows fat to coat each flour particle. The fat is cut up into small pieces and added to the flour. It is then rubbed in using the fingertips until the mixture resembles fine breadcrumbs. Water is then added to bind the mixture together before it is rolled out and used.

3. c) **Your answer should show *two* different methods:**
- Sketches should be 2D / 3D / cross section or a combination of these.
- Sketches should be clearly labelled.

Methods to describe and reasons given could include:
- Brushing with egg or milk to give a brown colour / improve appearance.
- Sprinkle with sugar to show it is a sweet product / improve colour / appearance.
- Add pastry decoration e.g. apple / leaves to improve appearance.
- Make the lid into a lattice, or pinch or fork the edges to improve appearance

Page 86

4. a) **Your answer should include *three* of the following:**
- Interview – face to face / telephone / video conferencing.
- Questionnaire.
- Survey – postal / on-line / e-mail.
- Taste panels.

4. b) **Your answer could include *four* of the following:**
- Type of pastry, filling and topping used.
- The shape, size, weight and colour of the pastry, filling or topping.

4. c) **Your answer could include *four* of the following:**
- You don't have to make anything, it is just a representation.
- It saves time and money.
- It can be used to predict what might happen.
- It produces accurate results.
- It can work out recipes and costs.
- It can show the effect of using different ingredients on the structure and nutritional profile of the product.
- It can show the effect of chilling, freezing or ambient temperature on bacteria.

Page 87

5. a) **Your answer could include *four* of the following:**
- To gather information about the product.
- To check salad against design specification.
- To produce nutritional analysis.
- To check recipe – ingredients/quantities.
- To modify the recipe to make improvements – check ingredients and quantities.
- To check cooking time of pasta.
- To ensure quality of salad.
- To conduct sensory analysis on taste/texture/aroma.
- To discover what consumers prefer.
- To compare new salad with existing salads.
- To evaluate sensory characteristics of the salad.
- To identify what improvements are needed.
- To produce a salad that will sell to the target group.
- To produce photographs for the packaging.
- To decide on packaging.

- To observe effects of storage on product and select most suitable storage method.

5. b) **Your answers should include *ONE* method only. The following points should be covered if relevant to your chosen method:**
   - Separate booths for testers so they aren't influenced by others.
   - Well lit, quiet area where they can't talk to others.
   - Dishes are randomly coded so testers can't identify them.
   - Food should be served in identical containers or plates.
   - Serve samples at the same temperature.
   - Use small samples.
   - Use coloured lights or blind folds if necessary.
   - Provide water or a plain biscuit to clear palate between tastings.
   - Provide clear instructions and have clear charts to fill in.
   - Give each tester the same quantity of food.

Page 88

5. c)

Area for Improvement	Adaptations
Tomato flavour	Add more tomato sauce. Use passata, tomato puree or tomato sauce. Add fresh tomatoes.
Spicy flavour	Use **fewer** spicy ingredients or remove one of them. Reduce weight of spicy ingredients e.g. mango chutney, curry powder.
Red colour of sauce	Add more red ingredients. Name them, e.g. red peppers, red apples, beetroot.
Firmness of pasta	Increase cooking time. Change type of pasta used. Check it is cooked correctly i.e. add to boiling water.

Page 89

6. a)

6. b) **The following points should be covered:**

Equipment	Name	Use
	Fluted cutters	Cutting out tarts, biscuits, sweet scones
	Baking tray	Holding food during cooking
	Grater	Grating food e.g. cheese, vegetables chocolate etc
	Food probe	Checking temperature of foods

- Follow manufacturers instructions.
- Avoid distractions.
- Equipment should be PAT tested and regularly checked and maintained.
- Don't have frayed or trailing flexes.
- Don't touch plugs with wet hands.
- Plugs must be correctly wired and fused.

Page 90

7. a) i)–iv) **Your answer should include *four* of the following:**
   - Can speed up manufacture.
   - Consistent outcome so each product is the same.
   - Can be bought in bulk.
   - Production costs are less.
   - Requires less skilled work force.
   - Less risk of cross contamination.

7. b) i)–iv) **Your answer should include *four* of the following:**
   - May be more expensive.
   - May have poor sensory qualities.
   - Time must be allowed for ordering and delivering.
   - May be delivery problems.
   - Other companies may use the same product.
   - Can't be modified.
   - Storage required.

8. a) i)–ii) Your answer should include *two* of the following:

Salmonella, Staphylcoccus aureus, Clostridium perfringens, Clostridium botulinum, Bacillus cereus, Escherichia-Coli (E-Coli), Listeria monocytogenes, Campylobacter.

Page 91

8. b) i)–iv) Your answer should include *four* of the following.

- Diarrhoea
- Headache
- Fever / temperature
- Abdominal pains
- Nausea
- Sickness / vomiting
- Mild flu-like symptoms
- Blood in diarrhoea
- Kidney failure
- Paralysis
- Difficulty breathing
- Double vision

8. c) Your answer should contain the following information, but not necessarily in this order. The more points you cover the more marks will be awarded. Give detail in your answer:

- High risk foods are easily contaminated by bacteria and so can cause food poisoning if not correctly stored at a temperature of 0–5°C and cooked thoroughly. They have a short shelf life.
- High risk foods include foods which aren't cooked before being eaten so, if contaminated, bacteria will not be destroyed e.g. cream, cooked meats, raw fish (sushi).
- Protein foods such as meat, milk, fish and eggs are high risk, as are cooked rice and lentils.
- Other high risk foods are moist foods like gravy and soup and unpasteurised foods e.g. soft cheese made from unpasteurised milk.

Page 92

8. d) You should include the following points in your answer:

- Ensure that the probe is clean by using an anti-bacterial wipe before and after use.
- Before use check that the temperature has been reset to 0°C.
- Check the centre (or thickest part) of the chicken with the probe.
- Check that the temperature has reached 72°C for at least 2 minutes.

8. e) You should include the following points in your answer:

- List the colour codes used on knives and boards and say which food is prepared using each one.

Colour	Use
White	Bakery and dairy products
Red	Raw meat
Blue	Raw fish
Green	Salads and fruits
Yellow	Cooked meat
Brown	Raw vegetables

- It prevents cross-contamination. You could include examples here.
- It means that different foods can be prepared without contacting each other and spreading bacteria.
- High risk foods are kept away from other foods, avoiding bacterial contamination.

Page 93

8. f)

	Type of Protective Clothing
Head and face	Hair net Moustache guard Beard net Eye protection if appropriate
Hand and arms	Disposable gloves Sleeve protectors Rubber gloves Chainmail gloves
Feet	Clean footwear Rubber boots
Body	Aprons Overalls Jacket White Coat

8. g) i)–iv) Your answer should include *four* of the following:

- Food hygiene training.
- Sanitise, clean hands.
- Short nails, no nail varnish.
- Blue plasters with a metal strip.
- Never lick spoons.
- Use correct equipment e.g. chopping boards.
- Wash hands after going to the toilet, blowing nose, coughing.
- Don't cough, sneeze, smoke near food.
- Don't pick spots and scabs.

Page 94

9. a) i)–ii) Your answer should include *two* of the following:

- Large quantities can be made efficiently.
- Production is completed by one person or team.
- Equipment can be adapted for different products.

9. b) Your answer should include *two* of the following:

- Products can be made 24 hours a day, seven days a week.
- Needs semi-skilled or unskilled workers and a smaller workforce so production costs are less.
- Large quantities can be made.
- It is accurate at producing consistent products.
- Machinery carries out hazardous processes reducing the risk of injury to workers.

9. c) i)–ii) Your answer should include *two* of the following:

- Individual 'special' products can be made.
- Prototypes can be produced.
- Doesn't need specialised equipment.

9. d)

Sensor	Use
Weight load	To weigh out ingredients To check weight of finished products
Temperature sensor	Maintain temperature within a given tolerance e.g. in cooking, cooling, chilling, freezing
pH level sensor	Tests acidity level
Electronic eye	Counts the number of a product
Metal detector	Detects presence of metal in a product at all stages of production and packaging

Page 95

10. Your answers should contain the following information:

10. a) i)

- It prevents food poisoning, which is a risk if it is eaten after the use-by date.
- It gives information because the consumer knows not to eat it as its safety is not guaranteed.
- It is a legal requirement to place this on high-risk foods which have a short shelf-life.

10. a) ii)

- The food can be eaten after the date given but the taste, texture or appearance may have deteriorated, e.g. crisps.
- It is a legal requirement and warns consumers about low-risk foods, e.g. canned foods.
- The food may be eaten after the date without the risk of food poisoning.

10. a) iii)

- This tells the retailer to remove it from the shelf.
- It helps the retailer with stock rotation.

10. a) iv) Informs the consumer that it doesn't contain gluten so that coeliacs would know it is safe to eat.

10. a) v) Warns the consumer that a very small amount of nut may be in the product or may have accidentally been in contact with it if the food is processed where nuts have been used previously. People with nut allergies know to avoid this product as a severe reaction may result in death.

10. b) In descending order of weight, with the largest listed first and the smallest listed last.

10. c) Trading Standards Officer

Page 96

11. A good high scoring answer would include:

- Food is packaged to protect it from physical harm (damage) when being handled, transported and displayed e.g. biscuits may be in a moulded plastic container then in a box which is shrink wrapped.
- To contain products e.g. soup is contained in a tin.
- To prevent tampering at any point in transportation, storage and at the point of sale.
- Preserves and extends shelf life, e.g. jam.
- Identifies e.g. labels on packets. You could give the details of any information found on labels, e.g. 'smoked' bacon, or has a picture of the product.
- Attracts customers – using colour, shape, size.
- Advertises the product so that consumers will buy it.
- Informs – gives details e.g. manufacturer, product name, ingredients, nutritional information.

12. a) This is the distance travelled by food from where it is produced to where it is eaten.

12. b) To reduce CO_2 emissions from the fuel used in transportation because CO_2 contributes to global warming by damaging the ozone layer.

12. c) **Your answer could include:**

- Use food in season.
- Use local food markets.
- Use local and regional products.
- Choose food from sources nearest the UK.

12. d) **Your answer could include:**

- Reduce the total amount used.
- Use CAD to produce packaging which protects and contains using minimal amounts of materials.
- Use recyled materials e.g. plastic.
- Use biodegradable materials e.g. paper.
- Use materials from sustainable resources, avoiding deforestation.
- Avoid wasting food that goes into landfill sites producing methane gas.
- Recycle used packaging.
- Use less colour on packaging as this uses chemicals.

ACKNOWLEDGEMENTS

The author and publisher are grateful to the copyright holders for permission to use quoted materials and images.

p.11   ©2009 Jupiterimages Corporation

Published by Lonsdale
An imprint of HarperCollins*Publishers*
77–85 Fulham Palace Road
London W6 8JB

© 2009 Lonsdale

ISBN 978-1-906415-48-8

First published 2009

01/061210

British Library Cataloguing in Publication Data.

A CIP record of this book is available from the British Library.

Book concept and development: Helen Jacobs
Commissioning Editor: Rebecca Skinner
Author: Judi Sunderland, Janet Inglis
Project Editor: Emma Rae
Cover Design: Angela English
Inside Concept Design: Helen Jacobs and Sarah Duxbury
Text Design and Layout: FiSH Books
Artwork: Lonsdale
Printed in the UK

Mixed Sources
Product group from well-managed forests and other controlled sources
www.fsc.org Cert no. SW-COC-001806
© 1996 Forest Stewardship Council

FSC is a non-profit international organisation established to promote the responsible management of the world's forests. Products carrying the FSC label are independently certified to assure consumers that they come from forests that are managed to meet the social, economic and ecological needs of present and future generations.

Find out more about HarperCollins and the environment at
www.harpercollins.co.uk/green

This booklet contains the answers for all the questions in the new GCSE Food Technology Essentials Workbook from Lonsdale.

Buy online at
www.lettsandlonsdale.com

9781906415471

□ get better results

ISBN 978-1-906415-48-8

9 781906 415488

Sustainable reading
www.harpercollins.co.uk/green

FSC + HarperCollins
Your choice makes a difference

www.lettsandlonsdale.com

£1.99

Judi Sunderland • Janet Inglis

ESSENTIALS

GCSE Design & Technology
Food Technology
Workbook

Contents

Eating for Health

4 Eating for Health
8 Proteins
10 Fats
11 Carbohydrates
12 Vitamins
13 Minerals and Water

Factors Affecting Customer Choice

14 Medical Factors
16 Food Allergies and Intolerance
17 Religion and Ethics
18 Ethics
20 Environmental and Social Issues

Cooking with Food

22 Meat
23 Fish
24 Milk
25 Milk Products
26 Cereals, Fruit and Vegetables
27 Eggs
28 Fats and Oils
29 Sugar

Functional Properties of Food

30 Functional Properties of Food
33 Effect of Acids and Alkalis on Food
34 Raising Agents
36 Cooking Food
37 Cakes
38 Pastry
39 Bread
40 Sauces
41 Modifying Basic Recipes

Contents

Making Food Safe

42 Enzymes
43 Yeasts and Moulds
44 Bacteria
45 Food Poisoning
46 Conditions for Bacterial Growth
48 Food Hygiene
49 Extending Shelf Life
50 Low Temperatures
52 High Temperature Methods
53 Additives

Designing Food Products

54 Designing Food Products
55 The Design Process
56 Specifications
59 Research
60 Computers: Research and Design
61 Computer Aided Design
62 Equipment
64 Sensory Analysis
67 Flow Charts

Food Manufacturing

68 Scales of Production
69 Computer Aided Manufacture
70 Quality Assurance and Quality Control
72 HACCP
74 Food Labelling
76 Packaging
78 Exam Style Questions

Eating for Health

Our Diet

1 Dietary Reference Values are guidelines about which of the following? Tick the correct option.

   A The amount of food to be eaten each day. ⬭

   B The percentage of nutrients in all foods. ⬭

   C The correct amount of nutrients and energy needed by different people. ⬭

   D The amount of nutrients needed by everybody. ⬭

The Eatwell Plate

2 Circle the correct options in the following sentences.

   a) You should choose food and drinks **high / low** in fat every day.

   b) Fruit and vegetables **are / aren't** essential for a healthy diet.

   c) A portion of fruit is approximately **3 tsp / 3 tbsp**.

   d) You **should / shouldn't** eat dairy products each day.

3 The Eatwell plate isn't suitable for which of the following groups of people? Tick the correct options.

   A People under medical supervision ⬭   **B** People who do a lot of sport ⬭

   C Children under the age of two ⬭   **D** People with special dietary needs ⬭

A Healthy Diet

4 Choose the correct words from the options given to complete the following sentences.

      saturated   **eating**   **healthy**   **increasing**   **sugar**

A .... diet shouldn't be boring. You should be able to achieve healthy

.... by cutting down on fat especially .... fat, salt,

...., and .... fibre (NSP).

5 Some manufacturers have voluntarily adopted a system of traffic light labelling. Below are the descriptions of each traffic light. Match the descriptions **A, B, C** with the traffic lights **1, 2, 3**. Enter the appropriate number in the boxes provided.

   A The amount is neither high nor low ⬭

   B The amount is low, this is a good choice to make ⬭

   C The amount is high, eat occasionally ⬭

Traffic light	
1	Red
2	Amber
3	Green

Eating for Health

Maintaining a Healthy Weight

1 Choose the correct words from the options given to complete the following sentences.

more **physical** **obese** **maintain** **needs** **seriously** **controlled**

increases **balancing** **overweight**

By .... the calories you eat with the .... exercise you take,

you can .... a healthy weight. If you eat .... calories than

your body .... you will become .... You should follow a

calorie .... diet, which limits calorie intake. If your weight

.... to a point where it .... endangers your health, you may

become ....

2 Why are the Food Standards Agency and the Department of Health working together?

....

3 Which of the following health problems are caused by obesity? Tick the correct options.

  A Some cancers ◯   **B** Constipation ◯

  C Coronary Heart Disease (CHD) ◯   **D** Type 2 diabetes ◯

  E Osteoarthritis ◯   **F** Acne ◯

  G High blood pressure ◯

Healthy Weight, Healthy Lives

4 What is the government strategy Healthy Weight, Healthy Lives trying to do?

....

5 Which of the following isn't an aim of Healthy Weight, Healthy Lives? Tick the correct option.

  A To support people to have a healthy diet and active lifestyle. ◯

  B To increase individual wealth. ◯

  C To increase life expectancy. ◯

  D To reduce the cost of treating health problems related to obesity. ◯

Eating for Health

Healthy Options

1 Which of the following are valid reasons for manufacturers producing healthy option foods? Tick the correct options.

    A The government say they have to. ☐

    B People won't buy any other food. ☐

    C They know people will buy them. ☐

    D They have the ingredients in stock. ☐

    E Many consumers are concerned about healthy eating. ☐

    F It will increase their profits. ☐

2 Why is it important for consumers to understand the claims made on labels?

_____

_____

3 Circle the correct options in the following sentences.

    a) Low salt products must contain **less / more** than 0.3g of salt per 100g.

    b) Too much salt in the diet will cause **high blood pressure / dental caries**.

    c) Products with **less / more** than 3.0g fat would be labelled low fat.

    d) Products labelled low sugar must contain less than **15g / 5g** of sugar per 100g.

    e) Too much sugar in the diet can lead to **dental caries / raised cholesterol**.

4 Which of the following health problems isn't caused by too much sugar? Tick the correct option.

    A Dental caries ☐

    B Obesity ☐

    C High blood pressure ☐

Fortification

5 What is fortification?

_____

Nutritional Profiles

1 What does a nutritional profile show? Tick the correct options.

    A   The cost of a dish. ⬭

    B   The nutrients in a dish. ⬭

    C   The amount of the dish you should eat. ⬭

    D   The energy in calories. ⬭

2 How could you make a nutritional profile?

_____

Calories

3 Choose the correct words from the options given to complete the following sentences.

active	energy	calories	asleep	food	all	brain activity

Energy in food is measured in _____. Energy is used for _____

bodily functions, including _____ _____. Your body uses energy

even when it is _____. The more _____ you are the more energy

you will need. Pumping blood around the body requires _____. All the energy you

need comes from _____ and drink.

4 Match the calories used in one hour **A, B, C, D** with the activities **1, 2, 3, 4**.
Enter the appropriate number in the boxes provided.

    A   Approximately 510 calories per hour. ⬭

    B   Approximately 240 calories per hour. ⬭

    C   Approximately 120 calories per hour. ⬭

    D   Approximately 75 calories per hour. ⬭

	Activities
1	Watching football
2	Sitting at a computer
3	Walking
4	Running

Proteins

Function of Protein

1 Which of the following are functions of protein in the body? Tick the correct options.

A For energy ◯   **B** To aid growth ◯

C To aid repair ◯   **D** To prevent rickets ◯

Proteins in the Body

2 Choose the correct words from the options given to complete the following sentence.

essential   thousands   eleven   amino acids   protein   absorbed   diet

During digestion, proteins are broken down into ....

Twenty different amino acids are found in plant and animal ....

.... of amino acids may be joined together to make one type of protein. Amino

acids are .... into the bloodstream and made into new proteins. The body can

make .... amino acids from other amino acids. The remaining nine amino acids

have to be obtained from protein in the .... These nine amino acids are known as

the .... amino acids.

Sources of Protein

3 Which of the following have High Biological Value? Tick the correct options from the ones given.

A Eggs ◯   **B** Shellfish ◯   **C** Quorn ◯

D Quinoa ◯   **E** Milk ◯   **F** Peas ◯

G Meat ◯   **H** Soya beans ◯   **I** Pulses ◯

4 Which of the following are plant-based proteins that have Low Biological Value? Tick the correct options.

A Quorn ◯   **B** Soya beans ◯   **C** Cereals ◯

D Beans ◯   **E** Quinoa. ◯   **F** Pulses ◯

G Rice ◯

5 Why should you eat a variety of low biological protein foods together?

◯

....

Plant-Based Proteins

1 The following statements are all about plant-based proteins. Circle the correct options in the following sentences.

a) Plant based proteins are **cheaper / more** expensive to produce than meat.

b) Plant based proteins take **more / less** land to produce than meat.

c) They are **easy / difficult** to store.

d) They are produced **more / less** quickly than meat.

2 Match the alternative proteins **A**, **B**, **C** with the descriptions **1**, **2**, **3**. Enter the appropriate number in the boxes provided.

A TVP. ◯

B Tival. ◯

C Quorn. ◯

	Description
1	Produced from wheat and vegetable proteins, similar texture to meat
2	A mycoprotein related to the mushroom
3	Made from soya beans

Properties of Plant-Based Proteins

3 Choose the correct words from the options given to complete the following sentences.

manufacture   **versatile**   **meat**   **bland**

a) Plant-based proteins are .... and can be bought in different forms.

b) Plant-based proteins are .... so can be flavoured easily.

c) Colour can be added during .... as they are colourless.

d) They cost less than .... or fish.

Who Eats Plant-Based Proteins?

4 Which of the following are reasons for using plant-based proteins? Tick the correct options.

A Wishing to avoid using animal sources because of religious reasons. ◯

B Wanting food which contains all the essential amino acids. ◯

C Being conscious of 'healthy eating'. ◯

D Wanting a more varied diet. ◯

Fats

Functions of Fat in the Body

1 Choose the correct words from the options given to describe the four functions of fat in the body.

warm   **provide**   **soluble**   **protect**

a) To _____ energy.

b) To _____ the internal organs.

c) To keep us _____ ,

d) To provide fat _____ vitamins A and D.

2 What is the difference between fats and oils?

_____

Vegetable Fats (Oils) and Animal Fats

3 Where do vegetable fats come from? Select the correct options from the ones given.

A Fish	◯	**B** Rape seeds	◯	**C** Soya	◯
D Meat	◯	**E** Nuts	◯	**F** Olives	◯
G Dripping	◯	**H** Sunflower seeds	◯	**I** Lard	◯

Types of Fat

4 Why should you eat a low amount of saturated fat?

_____

_____

5 Which of the following are contain saturated fat? Select the correct options from the ones given.

A Sausages	◯	**B** Oily fish	◯
C Cream	◯	**D** Sunflower oil	◯
E Coconut and palm oil	◯	**F** Walnut oil	◯
G Avocado	◯	**H** Hard cheese eg Cheddar	◯

6 Which gas is bubbled through some fats to make hydrogenated fat?

_____

Carbohydrates

Functions of Carbohydrates

1 Choose the correct words from the options given to complete the following sentences.

cholesterol   **eliminate**   **energy**   **fibre**

Carbohydrates have several uses in the body. They help to _____ waste products as

NSP, known as _____ , can't be digested. NSP reduces the _____

in the blood. Carbohydrates provide the body with _____ .

Types of Carbohydrates

2 Match the type of carbohydrate **A, B, C** with the descriptions **1, 2, 3**. Enter the appropriate number in the boxes provided.

A Sugar ◯

B Starch ◯

C NSP (fibre) ◯

	Description of Carbohydrates
1	Not sweet and doesn't dissolve
2	Can't be digested, eliminates waste products from the body
3	Sweet and dissolves

Conversion of Carbohydrates

3 Circle the correct options in the following sentences.

a) Sugars provide **instant / delayed** energy.

b) Starches have to be digested into **proteins / sugars** before the energy is released.

c) If you eat more carbohydrate than you need it will be stored as **fat / sugar**.

d) Eating more carbohydrates than you need can lead to **obesity / dental caries**.

e) Sugar causes **tooth decay / osteoarthritis**.

4 Why do athletes eat starchy foods such as pasta before an event?

_____

_____

_____

Vitamins

1 Which of the following chemicals make up vitamins? Tick the correct options.

    A Hydrogen ☐   **B** Carbon ☐

    C Aluminium ☐   **D** Oxygen ☐

    E Mercury ☐

2 Circle the correct options in the following sentences.

    a) **Some** /**all** vitamins can be stored in the body.

    b) Vitamins should be eaten **weekly** /**daily**.

    c) To get the vitamins you need you should eat a **wide** /**small** variety of food.

    d) You **should** /**shouldn't** need to take vitamin tablets.

    e) Vitamins A and D are **water** /**fat** soluble.

3 Which of the following isn't a function of vitamins? Tick the correct option.

    A Prevent illness and maintain good health ☐

    B Protect the internal organs ☐

    C Aid building and repair ☐

    D Control the release of energy needed by the body ☐

4 Choose the correct words from the options given to complete the following sentences.

    water   B complex   vitamin C   spina bifida   poisonous   orange

                             sunlight   eyes

    a) Folic acid prevents _____ in babies.

    b) Vitamin A is needed for healthy _____ and bone growth.

    c) Vitamins B and C are _____ soluble.

    d) Wholegrain cereals contain _____ vitamins.

    e) Too much vitamin D can be _____.

    f) Vitamin D can be produced by the action of _____ on the skin.

    g) Slow healing of wounds can show a deficiency of _____.

    h) Too much vitamin A may produce an _____ tint to the skin.

Minerals and Water

Facts About Minerals

1 Which of the following are functions of minerals? Tick the correct options.

    A Controlling how the body works ◯   **B** Preventing constipation ◯

    C Building the body ◯   **D** Ensuring good health ◯

2 Match minerals **A, B, C, D, E** with their functions **1, 2, 3, 4, 5**. Enter the appropriate number in the boxes provided.

    A Calcium ◯

    B Phosphorous ◯

    C Sodium ◯

    D Fluoride ◯

    E Iron ◯

	Function
1	Protects teeth
2	Transports oxygen in the body
3	Strong bones and teeth, and energy release from food
4	Strong bones, teeth and blood clotting
5	Water balance, and nerve and muscle activity

3 Which of the following are caused by excess sodium in the diet? Tick the correct options.

    A Tetany ◯   **B** Liver damage ◯

    C Raised blood pressure ◯   **D** Heart disease ◯

    E Brown spots on teeth ◯   **F** Stroke ◯

Water

4 How much water is needed per day by an adult? ....

5 Choose the correct words from the options given to complete the following sentences.

death   **lubricated**   **fatal**   **constipation**   **urine**   **essential**   **dehydrated**   **control**

Water is .... for life. Without water the body becomes ....

Joints are .... by water. Drinking sufficient water prevents

.... Perspiration helps to .... body temperature. Dehydration

can lead to .... Excess water is normally excreted as ....

In some cases excess water can be ....

Medical Factors

Dietary Choices

1 Fill in the missing words to complete the following sentences.

factors　　　**ethical**　　　**dietary**　　　**choices**

People make _____ about food depending on many _____

including _____ and medical needs, religion and _____ reasons.

Food and Pregnancy　　　　　　　Edexcel • OCR

2 Why does a pregnant woman need the correct balance of nutrients?

_____

3 Which of the following are foods which should be eaten by a pregnant woman? Tick the four correct options from the ones given.

A　Foods rich in iron　　◯　　　　**B**　High sugar foods　　◯

C　Foods containing calcium　◯　　　**D**　Fried foods　　◯

E　Foods containing folic acid　◯　　**F**　High fat foods　　◯

G　Foods with a lot of salt　◯　　　**H**　Foods high in NSP　◯

4 The following sentences are all about the foods which pregnant women should avoid. Circle the correct options in each sentence.

a)　**Cooked / Raw** or partially cooked eggs can cause salmonella.

b)　**Excess / Insufficient** vitamin A can poison the baby.

c)　Vitamin A is found in **chicken / liver**.

d)　Undercooked meat can cause **miscarriage / small birth weight**.

e)　The baby's nervous system can be harmed by eating **sword fish / sardines**.

f)　**Pasteurised / Unpasteurised** milk can cause listeria.

Coronary Heart Disease　　　　　　Edexcel • OCR

5 Which of the following can help to lower cholesterol levels? Tick the correct options.

A　Reducing saturated fat in your diet　◯　　**B**　Taking regular exercise　◯

C　Eating more red meat　　◯　　　　　　**D**　Eating more fruit and vegetables　◯

Diabetes

1 Which of the following complications can result from diabetes? Tick the correct options from the ones given.

A Heart disease ◯

B Food poisoning ◯

C High blood pressure ◯

D Blindness ◯

E Dental caries ◯

F Problems leading to amputations ◯

G Kidney disease ◯

2 Choose the correct words from the options given to complete the following sentences.

healthy   **two**   **exercise**   **injections**   **maturity**   **insulin**   **diet**

a) Diabetics can't produce sufficient _____.

b) There are _____ types of diabetes.

c) Type one diabetes can be treated with insulin _____.

d) Type 2 diabetes is also known as _____ onset diabetes.

e) Type 2 diabetes can be treated with _____ and exercise.

f) To prevent diabetes you should take regular _____.

g) Eating a _____ balanced diet will help to prevent diabetes.

Lactose Intolerance   Edexcel • AQA

3 Circle the correct options in the following sentences.

a) Lactose intolerance is **uncommon / common**.

b) It is caused by a lack of **lactase / lactose**.

c) People with lactose intolerance can't break down the natural **sugar / starch** found in cows' milk.

d) **Soya / Goats'** milk can be used to replace cows' milk.

e) Lactase is a(n) **hormone / enzyme**.

4 Which type of milk can be used by people with lactose intolerance?

_____

◯

Food Allergies and Intolerance

Allergies

1 Fill in the missing words to complete the following sentence.

intolerances   **immune**   **serious**   **allergies**

All .... involve the .... system and are usually more

.... than food ....

2 Which of the following isn't a symptom of an allergy? Tick the correct option

A Coughing ◯   **B** Nausea ◯

C Sore eyes ◯   **D** Headache ◯

Nut allergies

3 Circle the correct options in the following sentences.

a) In some people with a nut allergy, a very **large / small** trace is needed to trigger anaphylaxis.

b) Anaphylaxis is a **mild / severe** allergic reaction.

c) Anaphylaxis causes swelling of the **airways / eyes**.

d) Anaphylaxis causes **raised / lowered** blood pressure.

e) Anaphylaxis may result in **headache / death**.

f) Anaphylaxis must be treated with an injection of **adrenaline / insulin**.

Coeliac Disease   Edexcel • AQA

4 What is coeliac disease?

....

....

5 Which of the following can be caused by coeliac disease? Tick the correct options.

A Bone disease ◯   **B** Heart disease ◯

C Certain cancers ◯   **D** Diabetes ◯

E Growth problems in children ◯

Religion and Ethics

Religion

1 Match the religions **A, B, C, D** with dietary requirements **1, 2, 3, 4**.
Enter the appropriate number in the boxes provided.

A Sikhism ◯

B Islam ◯

C Hinduism ◯

D Judaism ◯

	Dietary requirements
1	No shellfish or pork. Only kosher meat
2	No beef, or beef products
3	No beef, may be vegetarian
4	No pork. Only halal meat

2 What is 'kosher' and 'halal' meat?

....

Ethical issues

3 Choose the correct words from the options given to complete the following sentence.

religious   **avoid**   **health**   **environment**   **meat**

People .... eating .... because of their

.... beliefs, concern about the .... and associated

.... risks.

4 Which of the following are used to prevent fish stocks running out? Tick the correct options from the ones given.

A Stop selling fish ◯

B Regulate the way fish are caught ◯

C Limit the amount of fish people can buy ◯

D Use fish farms to breed fish ◯

E Restrict fishing boats to a certain number of days a year ◯

5 Why is prawn fishing energy expensive and wasteful?

....

....

Ethics

Vegetarians and Vegans

1 Which of the following foods would be eaten by a vegetarian? Tick the correct options.

A Walnuts ◯ B Apples ◯ C Prawns ◯

D Cereals ◯ E Chicken ◯ F Baked beans ◯

G Bread ◯ H Potatoes ◯

2 What is the difference between vegetarian and vegan diets?

....

....

3 Which of these products will a vegan not eat? Tick the correct option.

A Brazil nuts ◯ B Apricots ◯

C Honey ◯ D Baked beans ◯

Organic Farming   Edexcel • OCR

4 Circle the correct options in the following sentences.

a) Organic foods are produced **with / without** the use of chemicals.

b) Organic foods **do / don't** include genetically modified crops.

c) The market for organic foods is **expanding / shrinking**.

d) There is **conclusive / inconclusive** evidence to show organic food is more nutritious.

e) People choose organic foods because they are concerned about **religious / ethical** issues.

5 Choose the correct words from the options given to complete the following sentences.

greenhouse   soil   wildlife   energy   lower

a) Organic production improves .... quality.

b) Organic farming reduces .... consumptions.

c) Organic farming doesn't contribute to .... gas emissions.

d) .... is increased by organic farming.

e) Organic farming can lead to .... carbon dioxide emissions.

The Red Tractor

1 The Red Tractor symbol assures consumers that food has reached agreed standards for what? Tick the correct options.

A Animal health ○

B Price ○

C No chemicals have been used ○

D Organic production ○

E Environmental issues ○

F Equipment used in production ○

G Responsible use of pesticides ○

2 Who is responsible for checking the Red Tractor standards?

....

....

Global Dimensions

3 Choose the correct words from the options given to complete the following sentence.

farmers   **fair**   **guarantees**   **independent**   **economically**

Fair trade is an .... consumer label which .... that the

.... and workers in lesser .... developed countries receive a

.... price for their goods.

4 From which of the following countries do Fair Trade products come? Tick the correct options.

A Asia ○

B America ○

C Caribbean ○

D Africa ○

Genetically Modified (GM) Foods

5 Circle the correct options in the following sentences.

a) Genetically modified foods have had their DNA **saved / altered**.

b) GM foods **are / aren't** always possible to identify.

c) GM crops can be developed which need **more / less** water.

d) GM crops can be grown to be disease **resistant / reliant**.

e) GM crops will be **less / more** important in feeding the world in the future.

Environmental and Social issues

Environmental Problems

1 Choose the correct words from the options given to complete the following sentence.

solve　　　　**national**　　　　**problems**　　　　**planning**

Environmental .... are a local, ... and global issue, and

co-ordinated .... is needed to .... them.

Reducing Food Miles

2 What is meant by 'food miles'? ....

3 How can you reduce food miles? Tick the correct options.

    A Buy food in season　　　　　　　　　　　　　　　⬭

    B Choose from sources near to the UK　　　　　　⬭

    C Use local or regional produce　　　　　　　　　⬭

    D Buy food which has been transported by air　⬭

    E Use local food markets　　　　　　　　　　　　⬭

4 Why is it important to buy some foods from other parts of the world?

....

Producing Less Waste and Recycling

5 Lorries, boats and planes are used to transport food. Which gas do they produce?

....

6 Circle the correct options in the following sentences.

    a) Food manufacturers are being encouraged to use **more / less** packaging.

    b) You can help produce less rubbish by buying food with **minimal / maximum** packaging.

    c) Recycling can save **energy / time**.

    d) Recycling **reduces / increases** greenhouse gas emissions.

    e) Waste in landfill sites produces **ethane / methane** gas.

Environmental and Social Issues

Avoiding Deforestation

1 Choose the correct words from the options given to complete the following sentences.

palm	global	animals	CO₂	biscuits	remove

a) Trees .... carbon dioxide from the atmosphere.

b) If large forest areas are cut down .... builds up.

c) Carbon dioxide contributes to .... warming.

d) Producing .... oil contributes to rain forests being cut down.

e) Palm oil is used in products like cakes and ....

f) .... that live in the rainforest are in danger of becoming extinct.

Reducing Carbon Dioxide Emissions

2 What causes global warming? ....

....

Eating Less Beef and Lamb

3 Fill in the missing words to complete the following sentences.

entire	methane	chicken	twenty	GHG	cows	lamb	harmful

Livestock, especially .... , produce .... gas which is

.... times more .... than CO₂. They produce more

.... than the .... world's transport. You should try eating

more .... and pork than beef or ....

4 Which of these foods is the **least** harmful to the environment? Tick the correct option.

A   Beefburger ⬭   B   Chicken sandwich ⬭

C   Roast lamb ⬭   D   Beef casserole ⬭

Meat

Sources of Meat

1 Choose the correct words from the options given to complete the following sentences.

animals   liver   carcass   meat   poultry   offal

a) Mechanically recovered meat is made by blasting the .... against a sieve.

b) Offal includes the internal organs such as ....

c) Turkey and chicken are examples of ....

d) Pork is a .... produced from pigs.

Cooking Meat

2 Which of the following are reasons for cooking meat? Tick the correct options.

A To make it tender ◯   **B** To make a special dish ◯

C To kill bacteria ◯   **D** To make it easier to digest ◯

3 Match the method of tenderising **A, B, C, D** with the description **1, 2, 3, 4**. Enter the appropriate number in the boxes provided.

	Description
1	Add concentrated enzymes sold as meat tenderisers
2	Hang the meat to allow natural enzymes to act
3	Use an acid eg. wine, tomatoes, yoghurt
4	Mince or flatten with a mallet

A Marinating ◯

B Mechanical ◯

C Aging ◯

D Using artificial substances ◯

4 Describe two changes that take place when meat is cooked?

a) ....

b) ....

Storing Meat

5 Circle the correct options in the following sentences

a) Meat and poultry should be stored on the **top / bottom** of the fridge.

b) Store meat in a clean **sealed / open** container.

c) Keep raw and cooked meat **together / separate** to avoid cross contamination.

d) You can refreeze meat after it has been **defrosted / cooked**.

e) Meat defrosted in a microwave should be cooked **later / immediately**.

Fish

Types of Fish

1 Name the three main types of fish.

a) .... **b)** .... **c)** ....

2 Which of the following are examples of oily fish? Tick the correct options.

    A Herrings ⃝   **B** Coley ⃝

    C Trout ⃝   **D** Tuna ⃝

3 Match the type of fish **A, B, C, D, E** with the examples of fish **1, 2, 3, 4, 5**. Enter the appropriate number in the boxes provided.

    A Oily ⃝

    B Flat white ⃝

    C Round white ⃝

    D Molluscs ⃝

    E Crustaceans ⃝

	Examples
1	Crabs, lobster, prawns, shrimps
2	Cod, haddock, coley, whiting
3	Oysters, scallops, cockles, mussels
4	Herrings, salmon, mackerel, sardines
5	Plaice, turbot, halibut, sole

Preparing and Storing Fish

4 Choose the correct words from the options given to complete the following sentences.

    without   **poached**   **high**   **covered**   **sea**   **canned**

a) Fish is a .... risk food.

b) Fish should be .... and stored in the fridge.

c) A lot of fish is frozen at ....

d) Hot smoked fish can be eaten .... cooking.

e) Oily fish can be .... in brine or tomato sauce.

f) Fish can be steamed or .... without a coating.

5 Fish begins to coagulate at what temperature? Tick the correct option.

    A 75°C ⃝   **B** 100°C ⃝

    C 30°C ⃝   **D** 60°C ⃝

Milk

Milk

1 Fill in the missing words to complete the following sentences.

Milk mostly comes from _____ and has a layer of cream on top. It is

_____ by forcing the milk through tiny holes under great _____ so

the fat _____ break down and can't reform. Milk _____ quickly so

it is heat treated to extend its _____ life and kill _____ .

Primary Processing of Milk

2 Match the milks **A, B, C, D, E** with the descriptions **1, 2, 3, 4, 5**. Enter the appropriate number in the boxes provided.

A Semi-skimmed ◯

B Skimmed ◯

C UHT ◯

D Sterilised ◯

E Dried ◯

	Description of milk
1	Pasteurised with all of the cream removed
2	Heated to 132°C–140°C for 1 second then cooled rapidly
3	Water is evaporated leaving a fine powder
4	Pasteurised with some of the cream removed
5	Homogenised, bottled sealed and heated to 110°C for 30 minutes

3 Fill in the missing words to complete the following sentences.

a) There are _____ types of canned milk.

b) Evaporated milk has _____ evaporated off.

c) Condensed milk is evaporated milk that isn't _____ .

Lactose Intolerance   Edexcel • AQA

4 People with lactose intolerance can't tolerate which of the following milks? Tick the correct option.

A Rice milk ◯

B Cows' milk ◯

C Soya milk ◯

D Coconut milk ◯

Milk Products

Secondary Processing of Milk

1 Which of the following are types of butter? Tick the correct options.

A Continental ◯   **B** Salted ◯   **C** Clarified ◯

D Lard ◯   **E** Ghee ◯   **F** Soya spread ◯

G Unsalted ◯

2 Choose the correct words from the options given to complete the following sentences.

churning   solid   margarine   dairy   bacterial   fat

a) Secondary processing of milk produces other .... products.

b) Butter is made by .... cream.

c) Butter may be added to .... to improve its flavour.

d) Cream is made from the .... of milk.

e) Yogurt is made by adding .... culture to milk.

f) Cheese is milk in a .... form.

3 Which of the following isn't a form of cream? Tick the correct option.

A Crème fraiche ◯   **B** Whipping ◯   **C** Clotted ◯

D Ghee ◯   **E** Soured ◯

4 Choose the correct words from the options given to complete the following sentences.

coagulate   third   digest   separates   fat

Cheese is approximately one .... protein, ... and water.

When cheese is heated it melts and ....; the proteins ....

and shrink making the cheese difficult to ....

Storing Dairy Products

5 Where should dairy foods be stored?

....

....

Cereals, Fruit and Vegetables

Cereals

1 Which of the following statements about cereals are factual? Tick the correct options.

A Cereals are a valuable source of protein ◯

B Cereals are edible seeds of grasses ◯

C Cereals are high in fat ◯

D Cereals can be made into many different food products ◯

E Cereals contain a high proportion of starch ◯

F Cereals are high in sugar ◯

2 Match cereals **A, B, C, D, E, F** with the food products **1, 2, 3, 4, 5, 6**. Enter the appropriate number in the boxes provided.

A Barley ◯

B Wheat ◯

C Rice ◯

D Maize ◯

E Oats ◯

F Rye ◯

	Food Production
1	Long grain, Short grain, Risotto, Flakes, Breakfast cereals, Rice cakes
2	Rolled oats, Oatmeal, Breakfast cereals
3	Ryeflour, Crispbreads, Rye bread
4	Pearl barley, Barley water
5	Corn on the cob, Sweetcorn, Cornflour, Pop corn, Polenta, Tortilla chips
6	Flour, Semolina, Breakfast cereals, Pasta, Noodles, Couscous

Fruit and Vegetables

3 How can fruit and vegetables be preserved at home?

....

....

4 Choose the correct words from the options given to complete the following sentences.

liquid   **prepared**   **raw**   **lid**

a) Fruit and vegetables should be .... just before use.

b) Eat them .... if possible.

c) Use a small amount of ....

d) Use a .... on the pan.

Classification and Size of Eggs

1 Which of the following describes Class A eggs? Tick the correct option.

A Removed from shell and pasteurised. ◯

B Clean, fresh, unbroken shells. ◯

C Clean, fresh, out of shells. ◯

D Clean, unbroken shells, pasteurised. ◯

2 What sort of eggs are commonly used by manufacturers?

_____

3 Choose the correct words from the options given to complete the following sentences.

code   blunt   barn   smelling

a) All eggs sold in Britain must be marked with a _____.

b) Eggs may be free range, _____ or battery.

c) Eggs should be stored _____ end upwards.

d) They should be kept away from strong _____ foods.

Function of Eggs

4 At what temperature does coagulation of egg white take place?

_____

5 Circle the correct options in the following sentences.

a) Aeration is used in making **meringues / lemon curd**.

b) Egg yolks are used to **bind / emulsify** oil and vinegar in mayonnaise.

c) Binding food with egg **holds ingredients together / stops them absorbing too much fat**.

d) Heating eggs can be used to **thicken / enrich** foods.

Fats and Oils

1 Which of the following provide us with fats and oils? Tick the correct options.

A Avocados ⬭   **B** Apples ⬭   **C** Wheat ⬭

D Carrots ⬭   **E** Olives ⬭   **F** Trout ⬭

G Pigs ⬭

2 Choose the correct words from the options given to complete the following sentences.

| fridge | obese | room | liquid | solidify | needed | solid |

a) Fat is _____ at room temperature.

b) Oil is _____ at room temperature.

c) Fat should be stored in the _____ to prevent it melting.

d) Oil should be stored at _____ temperature.

e) Oils _____ in cold temperatures.

f) Some fat is _____ by the body.

g) Too much fat can cause you to become overweight or _____ .

3 Which of the following are liquid at room temperature? Tick the correct options.

A Butter ⬭   **B** Cream ⬭   **C** Suet ⬭

D Olive oil ⬭   **E** Rapeseed oil ⬭   **F** Lard ⬭

G Dripping ⬭

4 Why is there a demand for low or reduced fat foods?

_____

5 Circle the correct options in the following sentences

a) **Butter / Lard** is used in shortcake biscuits for the flavour.

b) When flour particles are coated in fat the texture becomes **hard / short**.

c) Aeration takes place when fat is **creamed / rolled** with sugar.

d) Adding fat to baked products like bread will **aerate / extend shelf life.**

e) Using yellow fats like butter in place of white fats such as lard will add **colour / shelf life** to the product.

Sugar

1 Which two plants are used to produce sugar?

a) .... b) ....

2 Which of the following **isn't** a sugar? Tick the correct option.

    A Muscavado ◯   **B** Molasses ◯

    C Demerara ◯   **D** Sorbitol ◯

3 Choose the correct words from the options given to complete the following sentences.

    bacteria   **break**   **decay**   **sticky**   **enamel**   **teeth**   **acid**

Plaque is a .... substance made up of .... which is found

on the .... The bacteria .... down sugar and produce

.... that destroy the .... of the teeth. If you eat too much

sugar this leads to tooth ....

4 Circle the correct options in the following sentences.

    a) Artificial sweeteners are **low / high** in calories.

    b) Bulk sweeteners are used in **smaller / similar** quantities to sugar.

    c) Intense sweeteners are used in **smaller / larger** amounts than sugar.

    d) Caramelisation occurs when sugar solution is **over / under** heated.

    e) When starch is cooked in a dry heat **dextrinisation / caramelisation** takes place.

Functions of Sugar

5 Which of the following are functions of sugar? Tick the correct options.

    A Aeration ◯   **B** Thickening ◯

    C Colouring ◯   **D** Fermenting ◯

    E Decorating ◯   **F** Binding ◯

    G Sweetening ◯   **H** Emulsifying ◯

Functional Properties of Food

1 Why is it important that designers understand the functional properties of food?

_____

Solutions   Edexcel • AQA

2 Which of the following are examples of solutions? Tick the correct options.

   A Sugar in tea   ◯   **B** Fruit juice   ◯

   C Brine (salt and water)   ◯   **D** Cornflour in water   ◯

3 Fill in the missing words to complete the following sentences.

A solution is formed when a liquid is dissolved in another _____ or a

_____ is dissolved in a liquid. Solutions will not _____ when left

to _____ .

Suspensions   Edexcel • AQA

4 Circle the correct options in the following sentences.

  a) Suspensions are formed when **solid / liquid** particles don't dissolve in a liquid.

  b) Starch particles **do / don't** dissolve in a liquid.

  c) If a sauce isn't **agitated / aerated** the solids fall to the bottom.

  d) Flour in milk is an example of a **solid / suspension**.

Gels   Edexcel • AQA

5 Fill in the missing words to complete the following sentence.

A gel is a _____ jelly-like substance. Gels are mostly _____ , but

behave like solids due to the _____ agent holding the liquid in place.

6 Which of the following are examples of gels?

   A Sugar in tea   ◯   **B** Jam   ◯

   C Lemon meringue pie filling   ◯   **D** White sauce   ◯

Functional Properties of Food

Smart Starches Edexcel • AQA

1 What are smart starches?

....

....

2 Which of the following foods **doesn't** use smart starches? Tick the correct option.

    A Low calorie salad dressings ⬭   **B** Jam ⬭

    C Instant noodles ⬭   **D** Packet instant custard mix ⬭

Emulsions Edexcel • AQA

3 Choose the correct words from the options given to complete the following sentences.

lecithin   **unstable**   **immiscible**   **stable**   **mix**   **separates**   **emulsifier**

Liquids that will not .... together are .... When shaken

together they form an .... emulsion which .... when left

standing. The mixture only remains .... if an .... is used.

.... in egg yolk is an emulsifier.

4 Which of the following are examples of emulsions? Tick the correct options.

    A Mayonnaise ⬭   **B** White sauce ⬭

    C Cake mixture ⬭   **D** Chutney ⬭

Foams Edexcel • AQA

5 Circle the correct options in the following sentences.

    a) Foams are made when **liquid / gas** is mixed into a liquid.

    b) Foam creates a **heavy / light** texture.

    c) **Meringue / Mayonnaise** is an example of a foam.

6 Which of the following isn't a foam? Tick the correct option.

    A Whipped cream ⬭   **B** Ice cream ⬭

    C Yogurt ⬭   **D** Swiss roll ⬭

Functional Properties of Food

Elasticity

1 Explain how gluten is formed.

....

....

2 Which of the following products is gluten found in? Tick the correct option.

A Oats ☐   **B** Wheat ☐

C Barley ☐   **D** Rye ☐

Plasticity

3 Which of the following would use the function of plasticity? Tick the correct options.

A Spreading butter or margarine ☐   **B** Frying ☐

C Rubbing in ☐   **D** Melting method ☐

Shortening

4 Choose the correct words from the options given to complete the following sentences.

liquid	gluten	cakes	starch	crumbly	flour	coating

Fats make .... and biscuits .... and melt in the mouth by

forming a .... around the .... and protein molecules in flour.

This stops the .... coming into contact with .... and helps to

stop .... forming.

5 Circle the correct options in the following sentences.

a) Shortening means **long / short** lengths of gluten are formed.

b) In bread the gluten strands are **short / long**.

c) Short strands make the product **crumbly / firm**.

d) Fat forms a coating around the **starch / sugar** molecules.

Effect of Acids and Alkalis on Food

Acids in Food   Edexcel • AQA

1 Choose the correct words from the options given to complete the following sentences.

cheese   **sour**   **curd**   **bacteria**

a) .... in milk naturally produce acid.

b) Milk becomes lumpy with a .... taste.

c) The lumps are .... and the liquid is whey.

d) Drained curds are made into ....

2 Which of the following are caused by acids in food? Tick the correct option from the ones given.

  A   Oxidation of fruit

  B   Thickening cream or condensed milk by adding lemon juice

  C   Adding a sharp flavour to salad dressings

3 Match the acids **A, B, C** with the effect **1, 2, 3**. Enter the appropriate number in the boxes provided.

  A   Citric

  B   Acetic

  C   Ascorbic

	Effect
1	Prevents crystallisation in meringues, preserves vegetables
2	Speeds up fermentation in bread making
3	Prevents oxidation in fruit, thickens cream or condensed milk

Alkalis and Food   AQA

4 What is the pH value range of alkalis? Tick the correct option

  A pH 8–14   **B** pH 5–7   **C** pH 1–6   **D** pH 6–14

5 Fill in the missing words to complete the following sentences.

Alkalis are used as a .... agent e.g. .... of soda. When you

.... them they produce sodium .... , ...

and carbon ....

6 Why is cornflour added to meringues?

....

Raising Agents

Raising Agents

1 Choose the correct words from the options given to complete the following sentences.

rise　　　**expand**　　　**mechanical**　　　**gas**

a) Raising agents work by incorporating a _____ into the mixture.

b) When you heat gases they _____, and _____, then escape from the mixture.

c) Raising agents may be added by _____ means, or included in the ingredients.

2 Which of these isn't a natural raising agent? Tick the correct option.

A Steam ◯　　　　　　　　　　**B** Yeast ◯

C Air ◯　　　　　　　　　　　 **D** Baking powder ◯

Natural Raising Agents

3 Match the gases **A, B, C** with the method of incorporation **1, 2, 3**. Enter the appropriate number in the boxes provided.

	Method of Incorporating Gases
1	Added as liquid, cooked at a high temperature
2	Added as yeast ferments
3	Mechanically added by whisking and sieving

A Air ◯

B Steam ◯

C Carbon dioxide ◯

4 Which of the following use steam as the main raising agent? Tick the correct options.

A Swiss roll ◯　　　　　　　　**B** Yorkshire pudding ◯

C Meringues ◯　　　　　　　　 **D** Choux pastry ◯

E Scones ◯

5 What kind of texture is created when steam is used as a raising agent?

_____

Raising Agents

Biological Raising Agents

1 What four conditions does yeast need in order to reproduce?

a) .... b) ....

c) .... d) ....

2 At what temperature is yeast most active? Tick the correct option.

A 6°C–10°C ⬭   B 25°C–32°C ⬭

C 12°C–14°C ⬭   D 25°C–28°C ⬭

Chemical Raising Agents

3 How do chemical raising agents work?

....

4 Choose the correct words from the options given to complete the following sentences.

strong   alkali   yellow   heated   soapy   gingerbread

carbon dioxide

Bicarbonate of soda is an .... It produces .... and

washing soda when .... The washing soda is dark .... with

a .... taste. It is used in cakes with a .... flavour like

....

5 What can be mixed with bicarbonate of soda to prevent the soapy taste? Tick the correct options.

A Vinegar ⬭   B Sour milk ⬭

C Sugar ⬭   D Cream of tartar ⬭

E Cornflour ⬭   F Lemon juice ⬭

Cooking Food

Why Food is Cooked

1 Choose the correct words from the options given to complete the following sentences.

palatability   digest   bulky   texture   preserve

Food is cooked to...

a) make it easier to ....

b) make it less ....

c) .... it

d) improve its ....

e) change flavour and ....

Transferring Heat

2 What happens to food when it is cooked using heat transference?

....

3 Match each method of transferring heat **A, B, C, D** with the descriptions **1, 2, 3, 4**. Enter the appropriate number in the boxes provided.

	Description
1	Electricity is converted by the magnetron
2	Waves travel in straight lines to the food
3	Molecules are heated and begin to vibrate faster, colliding with the next molecule
4	Takes place in air or liquid, as molecules get hot they rise and fall when they cool

A Conduction ⬭   **B** Convection ⬭

C Radiation ⬭   **D** Microwaving ⬭

4 Fill in the missing words to complete the following sentences.

Electricity is .... by the .... into microwaves. Microwaves

.... 5cm into the food. They make the water ....

vibrate, creating ...., which makes ....

Cakes

Making Cakes

1 Match each method of cake making **A, B, C, D** with the type of cake **1, 2, 3, 4**.
Enter the appropriate number in the boxes provided.

A Whisking ◯

B Rubbing in ◯

C Melting ◯

D Creaming / All-in-one ◯

	Cakes
1	Gingerbread
2	Swiss roll, fatless sponge
3	Victoria sandwich, buns
4	Scones, raspberry buns

2 Fill in the missing words to complete the following sentence.
Cakes can be modified by...

a) using _____ flour in place of white

b) decorating the _____

c) _____ with marzipan or chocolate.

d) adding _____ to the mixture.

Functions of Cake Ingredients

3 Circle the correct options in the following sentences.

a) Sugar is used to sweeten and **raise / colour** the cake.

b) **Dextrinisation / Caramelisation** of flour gives colour.

c) Creaming fat and sugar traps **air / flavour**.

d) Eggs provide **moisture / protein** which converts to steam on cooking.

e) Sugar **hardens / softens** the structure.

f) Flour gives **flavour / structure** to the cake.

Aeration

4 What does aeration mean? _____

5 Which of the following isn't a method of adding air to the mixture? Tick the correct option.

A Creaming fat and sugar ◯   **B** Folding in flour ◯

C Whisking eggs and sugar ◯   **D** Sieving flour ◯

Pastry

Making Pastry

1 Choose the correct words from the options given to complete the following sentences.

steam   **dextrinisation**   **binds**   **shorten**

a) Water _____ the dry ingredients together.

b) When the pastry is cooked _____ of the starch gives colour.

c) Fat is used to _____ the pastry.

d) Water creates _____, which helps the pastry to rise.

2 Which of the following are methods of finishing pastry? Tick the correct options from the ones given.

A Sprinkle with sugar ⬭   **B** Sprinkle with flour ⬭

C Brush with egg ⬭   **D** Form a lattice pattern ⬭

E Brush with milk ⬭

Using Pastry

3 Match the type of pastry **A, B, C, D** with the resulting products **1, 2, 3, 4**. Enter the appropriate number in the boxes provided.

A Shortcrust ⬭

B Choux ⬭

C Flaky / rough puff ⬭

D Filo ⬭

	Products
1	Baklava, samosas,
2	Quiche, jam tarts
3	Chocolate éclairs, choux buns
4	Vanilla slices, pie tops, sausage rolls

Ready Made Pastry

4 Which of these is a disadvantage of using ready made pastry? Tick the correct option.

A Reliable outcome ⬭   **B** May contain additives ⬭

C Quick to use ⬭   **D** Guaranteed quality ⬭

Main Ingredients in Bread

1 Which type of flour is used for making bread?

_____

2 What is the function of yeast in bread? Tick the correct option.

A To add colour ⬭   **B** To give flavour ⬭

C Raising agent ⬭   **D** Increase protein ⬭

3 Choose the correct words from the options given to complete the following sentences.

salt   framework   gluten   carbon   raising

a) _____ helps bread to keep its shape. It is found in flour.

b) _____ is used to give flavour to bread.

c) When the yeast reproduces it gives off _____ dioxide which makes the bread rise.

d) Flour forms the _____ of the bread.

Modifying Bread

4 Fill in the missing words to complete the following sentences.

Bread can be modified by altering the _____ and shape of the product. The type of

_____ can be changed to _____ or granary. The

_____ can be altered by adding _____ such as glace icing or

_____ seeds.

5 Match the modification **A, B, C** with the effect of modifications **1, 2, 3**. Enter the appropriate number in the boxes provided.

A Use wholemeal flour ⬭

B Add cheese ⬭

C Add dried fruit ⬭

	Effect of modification
1	Sweetens bread, increases NSP
2	Increases NSP; taste, texture and appearance are altered
3	Increases protein and fat content

Sauces

Sauces

1 What are sauces? ....

2 Choose the correct words from the options given to complete the following sentences.

sweet   **bind**   **nutritive**   **flavour**   **moist**

Sauces add .... to a dish. Sauces may be .... or savoury.

A dry dish can be made .... by adding a sauce. The ....

value of a dish can be increased by using a sauce. A very thick sauce can be used to

.... ingredients together.

Thickening Sauces

3 Why do manufacturers sometimes use modified starch?

....

....

4 Circle the correct options in the following sentences.

a) If a sauce isn't stirred the particles will **float / sink** and form lumps.

b) At 80°C the starch particles **break open / collapse** and release starch.

c) When the starch is released this is known as **emulsification / gelatinisation**.

d) The thickened liquid forms a **foam / gel**.

e) On cooling the sauce will **solidify / separate**.

Modifying Sauces

5 What would be the effect of modifying a sauce by substituting semi-skimmed milk for full fat milk?

....

....

Modifying Basic Recipes

Modifying a Basic Recipe

1 What is meant by 'modifying' a recipe? ....

2 What is the correct term to use when the quantities of ingredients are changed? Tick the correct option.

    A Altering the quantities ◯   **B** Increasing the ingredients ◯

    C Amending the recipe ◯   **D** Altering the ratio ◯

3 When chopping vegetables for a soup, which of the following pieces of equipment could you use? Tick the correct options from the ones given.

    A Liquidiser ◯   **B** Processor ◯

    C Hand blender ◯   **D** Rolling pin ◯

    E Chopping board and knife ◯   **F** Biscuit cutter ◯

    G Grater ◯

4 Choose the correct words from the options given to complete the following sentences.

    processor   **dressing**   **Quorn**   **circles**   **scone**   **cheese**

    a) To modify a meat dish for a vegetarian use ....

    b) To change sweet scones to savoury replace the sugar with ....

    c) Cut carrots into strips not ....

    d) Change the texture of a chunky vegetable soup by using a ....

    e) Alter a salad by adding a ....

    f) Change a shepherds pie by adding a savoury .... topping in place of potatoes.

5 Give two examples of layered foods.

    a) ....   **b)** ....

6 Name three toppings you could use to cover fruit.

    a) ....   **b)** ....   **c)** ....

◯

Enzymes

Controlling Micro-organisms

1 Choose the correct words from the options given to complete the following sentences.

moulds	hanging	change	harmful
blue	unpleasant	time	tender

All foods _____ over _____. These changes aren't always

_____ e.g. _____ meat makes it more _____

and the flavour of _____ cheese is created by _____. But food

eventually becomes harmful or _____ to eat.

2 Which of these is not a micro-organism? Tick the correct option.

A Yeasts ⬭   **B** Enzymes ⬭

C Moulds ⬭   **D** Bacteria ⬭

Enzymes

3 Choose the correct words from the options given to complete the following sentences.

ripen   cells   animal

Enzymes are catalysts found in _____. The enzymes break down

_____ tissues and plant tissues. This causes fruit to _____.

Oxidation or Enzymic Action

4 Match the methods of preventing oxidation **A, B, C.** with examples **1, 2, 3**. Enter the appropriate number in the boxes provided.

A Adding acid ⬭

B Blanching ⬭

C Preventing contact with air ⬭

	Example
1	Put carrots in boiling water
2	Cover potatoes with cold water until needed
3	Add lemon juice to fruit salad

Yeasts and Moulds

Yeasts

Revision Guide Reference: Page 51

1 What are yeasts?

_____

2 Which of the following describe yeasts and their uses? Select the correct options from the ones given.

A Used to produce Quorn ⬜

B Grow only on sugary foods ⬜

C Can't grow at low temperatures ⬜

D Spoil the taste of food but don't make it harmful ⬜

E Can survive in vinegar ⬜

3 How can yeasts be used in food production? Tick the correct options.

A Bread making ⬜   **B** Jam making ⬜

C Alcohol production ⬜   **D** Making blue cheese ⬜

Moulds

4 Circle the correct options in the following sentences.

a) Moulds are tiny plants found in the **soil / air**.

b) Moulds like slightly **alkaline / acid** conditions.

c) Moulds need **moist / dry** conditions.

d) Moulds **live at / are destroyed by** temperatures above 70°C.

5 Fill in the missing words to complete the following sentence.

Mould on food is a sign that it isn't very _____ or has been _____

stored. Some _____ cause _____ reactions and respiratory

_____ . A few moulds produce _____

which can make you sick.

6 Which of the following are made by using mould? Tick the correct options.

A Bread ⬜   **B** Quorn ⬜

C Wine ⬜   **D** Blue cheese ⬜

Bacteria

Bacteria

1 What are bacteria?

_____

2 Which of the following describe bacteria? Tick the correct options.

A Some bacteria are harmless. ⬭

B All bacteria are dangerous. ⬭

C Bacteria are used in cheese making. ⬭

D Some bacteria can cause food poisoning. ⬭

E Bacteria are added to milk to make yogurt. ⬭

F The blue veins in cheese are made by bacteria. ⬭

G Some bacteria can aid digestion. ⬭

High Risk and Low Risk Foods

3 Choose the correct words from the options given to complete the following sentences.

high **destroyed** **contaminated** **eaten** **cooked**

Foods which aren't _____ before they're eaten are _____ risk. If

these foods are _____ by bacteria, the bacteria will not be _____

before the food is _____ .

4 Which of the following are high risk foods? Tick the correct options.

A Cooked ham ⬭ **B** Sugar ⬭

C Eggs ⬭ **D** Gravy ⬭

E Cooked rice ⬭ **F** Chutney ⬭

5 Circle the correct options in the following sentences.

a) In food manufacturing high and low risk foods are kept **together / separate**.

b) Workers dealing with raw food wear **the same / different** coloured clothing.

c) Once food is **cooked / chilled** it is kept separate from raw food.

d) Workers in food manufacturing must make sure food is **safe / nice** to eat.

Food Poisoning Bacteria

Revision Guide Reference: Page 53

1 Which of the following are common symptoms of food poisoning? Tick the correct options.

A Nausea ◯ **B** Pneumonia ◯

C Vomiting ◯ **D** Diarrhoea ◯

2 Why should pregnant women avoid unpasterurised milk, soft cheese and pâté?

3 Which of the following food poisoning bacteria is found in incorrectly canned meat, fish or vegetables? Tick the correct option.

A Campylobacter ◯ **B** Salmonella ◯

C E. Coli ◯ **D** Clostridium botulinum ◯

4 Why should you always wash your hands after using the lavatory, blowing your nose or coughing, when preparing food?

5 Which of the following foods may carry Bacillus cereus? Tick the correct options.

A Dried pasta ◯

B Cooked rice ◯

C Gravy ◯

D Cooked pasta ◯

E Shell fish ◯

F Cooked potatoes ◯

Conditions for Bacterial Growth

1 Which of the following conditions are needed for bacteria to grow? Tick the correct options.

A Cold temperatures ◯   **B** Time ◯

C Dry conditions ◯   **D** Warm conditions ◯

E Acid conditions ◯   **F** CO_2 ◯

G Oxygen ◯   **H** Moisture ◯

2 What is the danger zone?

....

....

....

3 Match the environment **A, B, C, D, E** with the temperatures **1, 2, 3, 4, 5**.
Enter the appropriate number in the boxes provided.

A Chillers ◯

B Fridges ◯

C Storage of frozen food ◯

D Danger zone ◯

E Temperature at which bacteria and spores are destroyed ◯

	Temperature
1	1–5°C
2	121°C
3	3–63°C
4	1–3°C
5	-18°C

4 Choose the correct words from the options given to complete the following sentences.

solid   **drying**   **moist**   **remove**   **sugar**   **salt**

a) Bacteria like .... conditions.

b) To stop bacteria growing .... the moisture.

c) Moisture can be removed by ....

d) High .... content reduces the moisture available.

e) Adding .... removes water by osmosis.

f) Freezing turns the liquid to a .... , which makes it unavailable for bacteria.

◯

Conditions for Bacterial Growth

Time

1 Choose the correct words from the options given to complete the following sentences.

quickly	million	cooled	seven
cooked	rapidly	fridge	control

Bacteria multiply _____. One bacterium can become one _____ in

less than _____ hours. To _____ bacteria multiplying you should

eat food _____ after it has been _____. Food which isn't going to

be eaten should be _____ quickly and stored in a _____ or freezer.

pH Level

2 Why is vinegar used to preserve foods?

_____

_____

3 Which of the following use vinegar as a preservative? Tick the correct options.

A Pickled onions ◯　　　　　　　　**B** Chutney ◯

C Pickled eggs ◯　　　　　　　　　**D** Apricot jam ◯

Oxygen

4 Some bacteria need oxygen. How do manufacturers prevent bacteria accessing oxygen? Tick the correct options.

A Modified Atmospheric Packaging ◯　　　**B** Tight fitting lids ◯

C Vacuum packing ◯　　　　　　　　　　**D** Controlled Atmospheric Packaging ◯

Cross contamination

5 The following sentences are about cross contamination. Circle the correct options in the following sentences.

a) It occurs when raw food touches food that **will / won't** be cooked before eating.

b) Hands **must / may** be washed between handling cooked and raw food.

Food Hygiene

1 Which system do home economists follow to ensure food safety?

_____

2 Which of the following should you do to ensure food is prepared safely? Tick the correct options.

A   Remove all jewellery ◯

B   Wear a bandage over cuts ◯

C   Don't wear nail varnish ◯

D   Wear a blue plaster with a metal strip over cuts ◯

E   Wear a hat ◯

F   Wear a clean apron ◯

G   Wear a hair net to cover all hair ◯

Preparing Food Safely

3 Circle the correct options in the following sentences.

a) Clean equipment in **warm / hot** soapy water.

b) Throw away rubbish **at the end / immediately**.

c) Use **any / antibacterial** cleaner for work tops.

d) In industry, use **steam / warm water** to clean equipment.

e) Cool food **overnight / rapidly** before storing.

f) Use a **thermometer / probe** to check the temperature of food.

4 Match the colour of chopping board **A, B, C, D, E, F** with the food **1, 2, 3, 4, 5, 6**. Enter the appropriate number in the boxes provided.

A   White ◯

B   Red ◯

C   Blue ◯

D   Green ◯

E   Yellow ◯

F   Brown ◯

	Food
1	Salads and fruit
2	Bakery and dairy products
3	Cooked meats
4	Raw vegetables
5	Raw fish
6	Raw meat

Shelf Life

1 What is meant by 'shelf life'?

_____

_____

2 Fill in the missing words to complete the following sentences.

When foods like potato crisps are past their _____ by date they aren't

_____ to eat, but may not be in the best condition for the consumer to

_____ them. A wide variety of _____ methods and packaging

techniques are used to _____ the shelf life of food.

Methods of Extending Shelf Life

3 Which of these foods is not packaged in a modified atmospheric condition? Tick the correct option.

A Bacon ⬭   **B** Biscuits ⬭

C Smoked fish ⬭   **D** Fresh vegetables flown in by air ⬭

4 Which method of preservation must be declared on labels? Tick the correct option.

A Dehydration ⬭   **B** MAP ⬭

C Irradiation ⬭   **D** Vacuum packaging ⬭

5 Circle the correct options in the following sentences.

a) In MAP, air is replaced by another gas which **promotes / prevents** bacterial growth.

b) Irradiation **delays / speeds up** fruit ripening.

c) Vacuum packing **spoils / preserves** flavours.

d) Dehydration is the **removal / addition** of moisture.

e) Micro-organisms are destroyed by **low / high** temperatures.

Low Temperatures

Low Temperature Methods

1 What happens to bacteria at low temperatures?

....

....

2 Which of the following are low temperature methods of keeping food? Tick the correct options.

A Irradiation ⬭   **B** Chilling ⬭

C Freezing ⬭   **D** Cook-chilling ⬭

Chilling and Cook-Chilling

3 What is the shelf life of cook-chill products? Tick the correct option.

A 3 months ⬭   **B** 1 week ⬭

C 90 minutes ⬭   **D** 5 days ⬭

4 Choose the correct words from the options given to complete the following sentence.

five   **cream**   **cooled**   **90**   **short**   **ready**

a) Chilling is used for foods like sandwiches and .... cakes. The food is kept for

a .... time.

b) Cook-chilling is used for .... meals. Food is cooked and

.... to 0–3°C in .... minutes. Foods have a shelf life of

.... days.

Freezing

5 Commercial food is stored at what temperature? Tick the correct option.

A -18°C ⬭   **B** 1–3°C ⬭

C 18–29°C ⬭   **D** -18–-29°C ⬭

6 Why is it important to freeze products quickly?

.... ⬭

Low Temperatures

Chillers and Freezers

1 Choose the correct words from the options given to complete the following sentences.

| shut | sensors | recorded | checked | defrosted |

a) Seals around chillers and freezers should be _____ often.

b) Chillers and freezers should be _____ regularly.

c) _____ should be used to raise an alarm if the temperature rises in the freezer.

d) Doors should be kept _____.

e) Temperatures must be _____.

2 Why is it necessary to keep a record of temperatures in the chiller and freezer cabinets?

_____

At Home

3 What is the cause of most food poisoning? Tick the correct option.

A Poor hygiene in factories. ⬭

B Poor storage in supermarkets. ⬭

C Bad choice of foods. ⬭

D Poor transportation, storage and use at home. ⬭

4 Which of the following instructions should be followed at home? Tick the correct options.

A Eat cook-chill dishes within three hours of cooking. ⬭

B Don't re-freeze frozen foods. ⬭

C Cool left-overs quickly before storing. ⬭

Accelerated Freeze Drying

5 Circle the correct options in the following sentences.

a) Accelerated freeze drying is a combination of **chilling / freezing** and drying.

b) Food is placed in a **cooker / vacuum** under reduced pressure.

c) Food is heated and ice changes to **water / vapour**.

d) AFD food is **heavy / light**.

High Temperature Methods

1 Choose the correct words from the options given to complete the following sentences.

short   **(UHT)**   **shelf**   **15**   **some**   **time**   **130°C**   **months**

a) During pasteurisation liquid is held at high temperatures for a _____ time. Milk is

heated to 72°C for _____ seconds then cooled rapidly to below 10°C which extends its

_____ life for days. But it only kills _____ bacteria.

b) During Ultra Heat Treatment _____, liquid is heated to a very high temperature for

a short _____. Milk is heated to _____ for 1 second and this

extends its shelf life for _____.

Sterilisation

2 How long is milk held at a high temperature during sterilisation? Tick the correct option.

     A   10 seconds   ◯   **B**   72 seconds   ◯

     C   1 hour   ◯   **D**   30 minutes   ◯

3 Why does sterilised milk taste different from pasteurised or UHT milk?

_____

Canning

4 Circle the correct options in the following sentences.

a) Canning is a form of **homogenisation / sterilisation**.

b) Food can be sterilised then packed into **see-through / sterilised** containers.

c) Containers are sealed to prevent **re-contamination / tampering**.

d) Canned foods have a very **short / long** shelf life.

5 Which of the following are high temperature methods of preservation which can be done at home? Tick the correct options.

     A   Chutney making   ◯   **B**   Irradiating   ◯   **C**   Pickling   ◯

     D   Freezing   ◯   **E**   Jamming   ◯

Additives and E Numbers

1 Match the type of additive **A, B, C** with the description **1, 2, 3**. Enter the appropriate number in the boxes provided.

A Natural ◯

B Chemical ◯

C Synthetic ◯

	Description
1	Made by scientists eg aspartame
2	Have the same chemical structure as a natural additive but made in a laboratory
3	Beetroot juice as a red colouring

2 What does an E number mean?

....

....

Uses of Additives

3 Which of these additives don't have E numbers? Tick the correct options.

A Emulsifiers and stabilisers ◯   **B** Flavour enhancers ◯

C Flavourings ◯   **D** Preservatives ◯

E Colours ◯   **F** Thickeners ◯

G Natural flavourings ◯

4 Choose the correct words from the options given to complete the following sentences.

stronger   separating   set   calories   enzymic browning

a) Gelling agents are used to .... jams.

b) Flavour enhancers make natural flavours ....

c) Anti-oxidants slow down .... in fruit and vegetables.

d) Sweeteners have fewer .... than sugar.

e) Stablisers stop ingredients ....

5 Which additives have been linked to hyperactivity in children? Tick the correct option.

A Flavourings ◯   **B** Thickeners ◯

C Gelling agents ◯   **D** Preservatives ◯

E Colourings ◯

Designing Food Products

Lifecycle

1 Choose the correct words from the options given to complete the following sentences.

invention **food** **keep** **re-invented** **longer**

The lifecycle of a _____ product is the time from _____ to the time

it is no _____ made. Products are _____ so that consumers will

_____ buying them.

2 Which of these statements are correct? Tick the correct options.

A Foreign travel has created a demand for foreign foods.

B Consumers want to reduce their carbon footprint.

C Some consumers are concerned about the use of GM crops.

D People concerned about animal welfare will choose battery eggs.

E Organic meat comes from intensively reared animals.

F People choose seasonal foods because they are concerned about the environment.

G An increasing variety of food is available because of improved transport.

3 Circle the correct options in the following sentences.

a) Ingredients **can / can't** be sourced globally. A multicultural society has **decreased / increased** the demand for foods from other countries.

b) Consumers have more money, so want more **luxury / budget** foods.

c) **All / Some** producers sell locally sourced foods.

d) Concern for health has led to a demand for **reduced / increased** fat products.

e) Sourcing foods globally means a(n) **increasing / decreasing** variety of foods are available.

Designing Food

4 Which of the following are modifications of existing foods? Tick the correct options.

A Sticky toffee pudding and cheesecake

B Mars bar and mini Mars bar

C Chicken breast in cheese sauce and burger in tomato sauce

D Baked beans in tomato sauce and baked beans in chilli sauce

E Tomato soup and reduced salt tomato soup

The Design Process

Developing Products

1 Choose the correct words from the options given to complete the following sentences.

specification   **research**   **factors**   **launched**   **target**

Manufacturers identify specific _____ groups when they give a brief to a designer.

From the brief a _____ can be produced. Designers may be asked to consider other

_____. The design process will begin with _____. Final

modifications are made to the product before the product is _____.

2 Circle the correct options in the following sentences.

a) The **specification / brief** gives guidelines and ideas.

b) From this the food **product / design** specification can be produced.

c) In addition, the **manufacturer / designer** may be asked to consider other **factors / ideas**.

The Design Process

3 Which of the following are reasons for manufacturers needing to design new foods? Tick the correct options.

A   Manufacturers are bored with making the same thing. ⬜

B   Consumers feel that the existing product is unhealthy. ⬜

C   Sales of a product are beginning to slow down. ⬜

4 Which of the following statements is true? Tick the correct option.

A   The brief tells the designer exactly what to make. ⬜

B   The brief gives guidelines and ideas. ⬜

C   The designer receives the brief after manufacturing the product. ⬜

D   The brief follows the prototype stage. ⬜

Specifications

Types of Specification

1 The table contains the names of three types of specifications.

Match descriptions **A, B, C** with the specifications **1, 2, 3** in the table. Enter the appropriate number in the boxes provided.

	Specification
1	Design
2	Product
3	Manufacturing

A A specification used to show others what the product should be like. ◯

B A specification used to make sure all the products are identical and safe. ◯

C A specification used during the design stage. ◯

Design Specification

2 Which of the following statements is true? Tick the correct options.

A The design specification is used to show what the product should be like. ◯

B The design specification is used to make sure all products are identical. ◯

C The design specification is used during the design stage. ◯

D The design specification is used to make sure all products are hygienic. ◯

3 Choose the correct words from the options given to complete the following sentences.

initial   intended   guideline

The design specification is a _____ for designers. It is developed from the

_____ brief. It describes what the product is _____ to do.

4 Circle the correct options in the following sentences.

a) The designer and **consumer / manufacturer** work together to develop the design specification.

b) Designers **write down / look up** the specification.

c) The design specification helps designers make sure their ideas meet the needs of the **consumer / retailer**.

d) The design specification is written **before / after** the product has been designed.

Specifications

Product Specification

1 Which of the following statements describe the function of a product specification? Tick the correct options.

A The product specification is used to show what the product should be like. ◯

B The product specification is used during the design stage. ◯

C The product specification may include a photograph. ◯

D The product specification will give the shelf life. ◯

E The product specification is used to ensure the product meets the needs of the manufacturer. ◯

F Detailed instructions for manufacture are included in the product specification. ◯

G Food hygiene procedures are included in the product specification. ◯

2 Circle the correct options in the following sentences.

a) The product specification often includes a **sample / photograph**.

b) The product specification includes details of **packaging / transportation**.

c) The product specification includes **estimates / tolerances** for sizes.

d) The product specification gives details of **serving / storage**.

Manufacturing Specification

3 Which of the following statements describes a manufacturing specification? Tick the correct options.

A Measurements for sizes and volume are included. ◯

B The manufacturing specification is top secret. ◯

C The manufacturing specification is developed by the designer. ◯

D Where the ingredients come from is written in the manufacturing specification. ◯

E A description of the texture and colour is included. ◯

F Food hygiene procedures are included in the manufacturing specification. ◯

G The manufacturing specification is used during the design stage. ◯

H Detailed instructions for manufacture are included in the manufacturing specification. ◯

Specifications

Portion Control

1 Choose the correct words from the options given to complete the following sentences.

problem   **shape**   **identical**   **specific**

Portion control ensures that all products are _____. The size and

_____ of cutters are written into the specification. If too large a cutter is used it will

cause a _____. Wrappers are made to fit _____ sizes.

2 Why is it important that products are always the same size and shape? Tick the correct option.

    A To meet food hygiene regulations ◯   **B** It is a legal requirement ◯

    C So they fit in the packaging ◯   **D** So they can be exported ◯

Standard Components

3 Which of the following are standard components? Tick the correct options.

    A Pre-blended spice mixes ◯   **B** Pizza bases ◯

    C Carrots ◯   **D** Flan cases ◯

Standard Components: Advantages and Disadvantages

4 Which of the following statements are advantages of using standard components? Tick the correct options.

    A Standard components may be more expensive. ◯

    B Time must be allowed for ordering and delivery. ◯

    C Reduces risk of cross-contamination e.g. a sandwich manufacturer buys cooked
chicken instead of cooking raw chicken. ◯

    D Simplifies production so a less skilled workforce may be required. ◯

    E There may be supply problems. ◯

5 Fill in the missing words to complete the following sentences.

Standard components have some disadvantages. You must allow _____ for delivery

and there may be _____ problems. They may be more expensive or have poor

_____ qualities. You might find that other food _____

use the same _____.

Research

Researching

1 Choose the correct word from the options given to complete the following sentences.

didn't   someone   secondary   information   primary   collected   original

a) _____ research means collecting your own _____

information which _____ exist before.

b) _____ research means using _____ already

_____ by _____ else.

2 Which of the following are examples of primary research? Tick the correct option.

A Questionnaires ◯ **B** Recipe books ◯

C Surveys ◯ **D** Focus groups ◯

E Magazine articles ◯ **F** Leaflets ◯

G Disassembly ◯

Disassembly

3 What does disassembly mean?

_____

_____

4 During disassembly of a product, which of the following information can be found on a packet of samosas? Tick the correct options.

A Weight of filling ◯ **B** List of ingredients ◯

C Number of items in the packet ◯ **D** Finish to pastry ◯

E Length of samosas ◯ **F** Cost of the packaging ◯

G Depth of pastry. ◯ **H** Shelf life of the samosas ◯

Computers: Research and Design

Research Using Computers

1 The following are all ways in which computers can be used for research. Circle the correct options in the following sentences.

a) Computers can be used to **find / record** results of observations.

b) **Spreadsheets / Publisher** can be used to record results.

c) Using e-mails can **speed up / slow down** communication.

d) Information from questionnaires can be analysed using a **powerpoint / database.**

e) People in other parts of the country can be interviewed using **video conferencing / spreadsheets.**

Why Use Computer Aided Design?

2 Which of the following are advantages of using computers for designing? Tick the correct options.

A Mathematical work can be done quickly. ◯

B Modelling means designers don't have to make real dishes. ◯

C Mathematical work can be inaccurate. ◯

D Labels can be designed and changed quickly. ◯

The Internet

3 Which of the following is a reason for using a competitor's web site as part of research? Tick the correct option.

A To find the manufacturing specification. ◯

B To look at their products for disassembly. ◯

C To find out where they source their ingredients from. ◯

D To discover the recipes for their products. ◯

4 Fill in the missing words to complete the following sentences.

EPOS is used as part of research. As food passes through the .... in

supermarkets, a .... is built which shows how well a particular food product is

....

Computer Aided Design

Modelling

1 What is modelling?

_____

_____

2 The following statements are ways in which modelling can be used in designing. (Circle) the correct options in the following sentences.

a) To show the growth of **bacteria / enzymes** in different conditions.

b) To demonstrate changes to the **structure / taste** of food when changing ingredients.

c) To show the change to the cost of **manufacture / design** when changing ingredients can be shown.

d) To model the effect on the nutritional profile when changing **ingredients / suppliers** can be modelled.

e) Mathematical modelling shows how **costs / packaging** change when ingredients are altered.

3 Fill in the missing words to complete the following sentences.

Ideas can be modelled without having to _____ anything. Modelling is used to

_____ what happens when numbers change i.e. in a _____ .

Computers and Design

4 Which of the following are ways in which computers can be used during designing? Tick the correct options.

A   To control the temperature of refrigerators. ◯

B   To scale up recipes. ◯

C   To make real dishes. ◯

D   For modelling costs. ◯

E   For working out the nutritional profile of a dish. ◯

Equipment

Small Equipment

1 Choose the correct word from the options given to complete the following sentence.

prototypes   **money**   **test**

Designers make _____ in the _____ kitchen. Manufacturers use

electrical equipment because it saves time, labour and _____ .

2 Circle the correct options in the following sentences.

a) Using small equipment obtains **different / consistent** results.

b) Small electrical equipment guarantees the quality of the **recipe / outcome**.

c) Human error can be **avoided / guaranteed** by using small electrical equipment.

Safety

3 Which of the following should you do to prevent accidents? Select the correct options from the ones given.

A   Follow manufacturers' instructions. ◯

B   Switch off gas if a leak is suspected. ◯

C   Keep an open window near the gas hob. ◯

D   Use heat resistant gloves where necessary. ◯

E   Ensure plugs are correctly wired and fused. ◯

F   Make sure equipment has passed the PAT test. ◯

4 Choose the correct words from the options given to complete the following sentences.

train   **HACCP**   **industry**   **safely**   **operate**

In the food _____ , part of the _____ procedure is to

_____ workers. No one is allowed to _____ machinery until they

have been trained how to do so correctly and _____ .

5 Explain how to use a knife in the kitchen safely.

_____

_____

_____

Equipment

Equipment in Test Kitchens

1 Circle the correct options in the following sentences.

a) Home Economists in test kitchen use similar equipment to that used in **factories / schools.** ◯

b) Electric misers ensure that mixtures are mixed at **different / the same** speed. ◯

c) **Electric / Balance** scales are the most accurate. ◯

Computer Integrated Manufacture (CIM)   Edexcel • OCR

2 Explain what is meant by CIM.

3 The following statements describe the process for manufacturing biscuits using CIM. Put them in the correct order **1–8**.

A   The biscuits are packaged. ◯

B   The biscuits are cooled in a cooling chamber. ◯

C   The mixture is rolled out to the correct thickness by large rollers. ◯

D   The mixture is emptied onto a conveyor belt. ◯

E   The biscuits are taken on a conveyor belt to a tunnel oven. ◯

F   The mixture is cut out by shaped rollers. ◯

G   The mixture is weighed. ◯

H   The mixture is mixed in an enclosed container. ◯

4 Which of the following statements about CIM are true? Tick the correct options.

A   Throughout production the product isn't touched by a person. ◯

B   Mixing takes place in open containers. ◯

C   The ingredients are pumped through pipes. ◯

D   The ingredients are weighed using loading cells. ◯

Sensory Analysis

1 Choose the correct word from the options provided to complete the following sentence.

like	**analysis**	**five**	**food**	**senses**	**eat**

Sensory _____ involves using our five _____ to evaluate whether

or not we _____ a dish. We use all our _____ senses when we

_____ to give us information about _____ .

2 Which of the following are reasons for using sensory analysis? Tick the correct options from the ones given.

A Comparing food with other existing products. ☐

B Evaluating sensory characteristics of food. ☐

C To taste new things. ☐

D Improving future products. ☐

E To taste dishes you don't normally eat. ☐

F Identifying where improvements are needed. ☐

G Gathering information about the product. ☐

3 Which of these senses is used to test the texture of food? Tick the correct option.

A Sight ☐   B Hearing ☐   C Smell ☐   D Touch ☐

Conducting Sensory Analysis

4 The following sentences explain how to ensure a fair test. Circle the correct options in the following sentences.

a) Sensory analysis should take place in **controlled / noisy** conditions.

b) Use an area where the light **is dim / can be changed**.

c) Serve **large / small** quantities of food.

d) Serve food on **identical / different** dishes.

e) Write the **name / code** of the food on the dish.

5 Which of these are given to testers during sensory analysis? Tick the correct options.

A Clear instructions ☐   B Water or cracker to clear the palate ☐

C A large portion ☐   D Charts to complete ☐

Sensory Analysis

Using Sensory Analysis

1 When is sensory analysis used in developing a product? Tick the correct option.

    A   Only during evaluation.   ⬭

    B   At different stages of development.   ⬭

    C   During the research only.   ⬭

    D   Whilst writing the brief.   ⬭

2 Fill in the missing words to complete the following sentences.

Some sensory analysis testing needs to be done as part of _____ new dishes that

are being developed. The testing can be done by _____ testers or by members of

the public. It can take place in special _____ analysis booths, in public places and

_____ homes.

Techniques for Testing

3 Which of the following are types of tests that can be used to find out which products people like best? Tick the correct options.

    A   Paired preference test   ⬭

    B   Triangle test   ⬭

    C   Attribute test   ⬭

    D   Hedonic rating test   ⬭

4 Which test is being described here? 'Testers are given two samples of food and they have to indicate which they prefer'. Tick the correct option.

    A   Attribute testing   ⬭

    B   Hedonic Rating   ⬭

    C   A not A   ⬭

    D   Paired preference   ⬭

Sensory Analysis

Discriminatory Testing

1 Which of the following is a reason for using discriminatory testing? Tick the correct option.

    A To find out which product people prefer. ⬭

    B To build up a profile of a dish. ⬭

    C To see which of two samples consumers prefer. ⬭

    D To see if consumers can tell the difference between two samples. ⬭

2 The following statements are all about discriminatory testing. Circle the correct options in the following sentences.

    a) In A not A testing, testers are given one sample followed by **four /two** further samples.

    b) Discriminatory testing includes **attribute /triangle** testing.

    c) In triangle testing, testers are given **three /five** samples.

    d) In **A not A /triangle** testing, testers are given a control sample first.

3 Choose the correct word from the options given to complete the following sentences.

    control   **different**   **like**   **triangle**   **identify**   **two**   **identify**   **same**

    a) In .... testing, three samples are tested. Two samples are the

    .... and one is .... The tester has to

    .... the odd one out.

    b) In A not A testing, testers are given a .... sample to try. They are then given

    .... further samples. One of these is .... the control and

    one is different. They are asked to .... which one is like the control sample.

Attribute Testing

4 Which of the following are reasons for using attribute testing. Tick the correct options.

    A To build up a detailed evaluation to compare against the ideal. ⬭

    B To show if modifications are needed. ⬭

    C To see which product consumers prefer. ⬭

    D As part of disassembly of other dishes. ⬭

Facts About Flow Charts

1 What are flow charts?

_____

_____

2 Why do designers use flow charts? Tick the correct option.

A Because it is easier for them. ⬭

B To make sure that every time the product is made it is the same. ⬭

C To be able to use a computer to make it quicker. ⬭

D So no one else can copy it. ⬭

3 Match the names **A**, **B**, **C** with the three flow chart symbols **1**, **2**, **3**. Enter the appropriate number in the boxes provided.

A Terminator – used at the start or end of the system. ⬭

B Process – the activity that needs to be carried out. ⬭

C Decision – when a question has to be asked. ⬭

	Symbol
1	◇
2	⬭
3	▭

4 Choose the correct word from the options provided to complete the following sentences.

production   **quality**   **BSI**   **systems**   **make**   **manufacturer**

Flow charts show complex _____ in a simple diagram. They are all written using

standard _____ symbols. Designers work from flow charts to make sure that every

time they _____ the product it is the same. A flow chart also allows the food

_____ to set up a _____ line which will result in a good

_____, safe final product.

Scales of Production

Scales of Production

1 Fill in the missing words to complete the following sentences.

stored　　**shelf**　　**scale**　　**time**　　**waste**　　**make**　　**delivered**　　**predicted**

a) Manufacturers decide on the _____ of production depending on the number of

products _____ to be sold and the _____ life.

b) Just in _____ means that manufacturers make food just in time to be

_____ to customers so no food is stored. This cuts down

_____ and reduces risk.

One-Off Production

2 What is 'Jobbing' also known as? Tick the correct option.

A Mass production ⬭　　　　　　**B** Continuous flow production ⬭

C Batch production ⬭　　　　　　**D** One-off production ⬭

3 Which of the following statements refer to one-off production? Tick the correct options.

A It includes cakes for special occasions. ⬭

B It relies on Computer Aided Manufacture. ⬭

C Products are made 24 hours a day, 7 days a week. ⬭

D It is used by small scale manufacturers. ⬭

E Large quantities of food can be made efficiently. ⬭

Mass Production

4 Circle the correct word in the following sentences.

a) Small scale manufacturers use **continuous flow / batch production**.

b) One-off production relies on **unskilled / skilled** workers.

c) Equipment used in batch production **can / can't** be adapted for use.

d) **Batch production / Continuous flow** often relies on Computer Aided Manufacture.

e) Continuous flow production relies on **unskilled / skilled** workers.

Computer Aided Manufacture

Why Use CAM?

Revision Guide Reference: Page 81

1 What do the initials CAM stand for?

_____

_____

2 Which of the following statements are reasons for using CAM? Tick the correct options.

A It increases productivity. ⬭

B Labour costs are more expensive. ⬭

C It can assess thousands of products in minutes. ⬭

D It can detect things the human eye can't see. ⬭

E It's less hygienic. ⬭

F It doesn't make mistakes. ⬭

G It can run all day without a break. ⬭

How CAM is used in industry

3 The following statements describe some of the processes which use CAM. Circle the correct words in the following sentences.

a) To measure weight a **light detector / load cell** would be used.

b) The viscosity of a sauce can be checked by a **light detector / electronic eye**.

c) The presence of bacteria is detected by a **pH / micro-biological** sensor.

d) Colour changes can be detected by an **electronic eye / light refractor**.

e) The presence of metal in a package is detected by a **metal / light** detector.

4 Choose the correct words from the options given to complete the following sentences.

automatic	production	blown	remedial	computer
	pushed	alarm	control	

When the _____ detects a problem, appropriate _____ action is

taken. This might include _____ adjustment being made by the

_____ e.g. oven temperatures. In other cases it could include an

_____ flashing or the food may be _____ or

_____ off the _____ line.

Quality Assurance and Quality Control

Quality

1 What does quality mean? Tick the correct option.

A   It is expensive. ◯

B   It meets the customers needs. ◯

C   The product can be found in different sizes. ◯

D   The product is disposable. ◯

2 Fill in the missing word to complete the following sentences.

Consumers expect food to be _____ to eat, to always look and

_____ the same and to be the same size. If the food is _____,

you're more likely to _____ it again.

Quality Assurance

3 What can companies who reach high standards for delivering quality products and services gain?

_____

4 Quality Assurance is a term used by the food manufacturing industry. Which areas of work does it cover? Circle the correct options in the following sentences.

a) Designing a food to meet **consumers' / designers'** needs.

b) Meeting all legal requirements for **health / hygiene** and safety.

c) Sourcing and buying ingredients from **cheap / reliable** growers.

d) **Maintenance / Monitoring** of equipment.

e) **Quick / Safe** manufacturing processes.

f) Quality control **notes / records**.

g) **Safe / Attractive** packaging.

h) Customer **relations / relatives**.

Quality Assurance and Quality Control

Quality Control

1 Quality Control involves checking the quality of the product during which stages? Tick the correct options.

A During manufacture ☐   **B** At the supermarket ☐

C During design ☐   **D** At the end of manufacture ☐

2 Explain what will happen if a manufacturer produces a food which makes people ill.

_____

_____

_____

The 1990 Food Safety Act   Edexcel • OCR

3 Which of the following functions are carried out by Trading Standards Officers? Tick the correct options.

A To make sure no misleading claims are made. ☐

B To check weighing and measuring equipment. ☐

C To make sure food is made safely with no risk to consumers. ☐

D To give advice to consumers. ☐

4 Which of the following are Quality Control Points? Tick the correct options.

A Checking shape ☐

B Testing temperatures of meat storage ☐

C Ensuring sizes are within tolerance ☐

D Inspecting taste and texture ☐

E Checking for metal in mixtures ☐

F Making sure shapes are accurate ☐

G Checking quality of enrobing in chocolate biscuits ☐

H Checking for bacterial contamination ☐

5 What is done at the Critical Control Points?

_____

_____

☐

_____

HACCP

Hazards

1 What do the initials HACCP stand for?

_____

2 Fill in the missing words to complete the following sentences.

When a new product is being designed a hazard _____ must be carried out. This

means working out what could go _____ during manufacture in order to plan how to

_____ it happening. The system used in _____ manufacturing is

Hazard Analysis and Critical Control Point or _____ .

Types of Hazard

3 The table contains the three types of hazard in food production. Match the description **A**, **B**, **C** with the hazards **1**, **2**, **3**. Enter the appropriate number in the boxes provided.

A Contamination by cleaning fluids, pesticides or chlorine ◯

B Contamination by bacteria ◯

C Foreign bodies in the product eg metal from machinery ◯

	Hazard
1	Biological
2	Physical
3	Chemical

4 The following are stages when hazards can occur in food production.
Choose the correct words from the options given to complete the following sentences.

transportation   **manufacturer**   **reheating**   **harvesting**   **storage**

a) During growing and _____ raw ingredients.

b) Storage of the product by the _____ .

c) During _____ of ingredients.

d) _____ by the retailer.

e) Storage and _____ by the consumer.

5 Why does most food poisoning happen?

_____

_____

HACCP Charts

1 The following statements explain how to produce a HACCP chart. Choose the correct words from the options given to complete the following sentences.

problem   **risks**   **tolerances**   **processes**

removed   **monitored**   **critical**

a) List the manufacturing ....

b) Identify where the .... may happen.

c) Decide which are .... to the safety of the consumer.

d) Plan how the risks may be ....

e) Set .... for the controls.

f) Plan how the controls will be ....

g) Decide what to do if there is a ....

2 If raw meat was delivered at a temperature of 8°C what action should be taken? Tick the correct option.

    A Refrigerate to lower the temperature ◯

    B Use it quickly ◯

    C Refuse delivery ◯

    D Use it for cheaper products ◯

3 What is meant by FIFO and how is it used?

....

....

4 What basic qualification should all food industry workers have?

....

5 If the bread dough was insufficiently mixed what action should be taken? Tick the correct option.

A Discard the mixture ◯		**B** Mix it for longer ◯
C Refuse delivery ◯		**D** Mix it faster ◯
E Make a new mixture ◯		

Food Labelling

Labelling

1 Who controls labelling regulations?

_____

2 Choose the correct words from the options given to complete the following sentences.

understood	**language**	**legal**	**accurate**	**law**	**inform**

Some information on packaging is a _____ requirement (it has to be included by

_____). Labels must be in a _____ that can be

_____ in the country of use. Information on labels must _____ the

consumer and be _____ .

3 Which of the following is the job of a Trading Standards Officer? Tick the correct option.

A To make sure the price is on the label. ◯

B To check that labels don't describe food in a misleading way. ◯

C To check that the food is produced in the UK. ◯

D To make sure that the label has a bar code. ◯

Legal Requirements on Labels

4 Which of the following are legal requirements on a label? Tick the correct options.

A The country of origin ◯   **B** Name of the product ◯

C An illustration of the food ◯   **D** Ingredients list ◯

E Storage instruction ◯   **F** Nutritional information ◯

G Best-before or sell-by date ◯   **H** Manufacturers' name ◯

Voluntary Information on Labels

1 Fill in the missing words to complete the following sentences.

Food products use terms such as _____ fresh and wholesome which don't have

_____ meanings. These terms are used to _____ the food.

Manufacturers don't have to label foods as _____ for vegetarians but it is a selling point.

2 What does a batch or lot mark do? Tick the correct option.

A Allows the retailer to know how old it is. ◯

B Allows the consumer to find out where it was made. ◯

C Allows the food to be traced back to where and when it was produced. ◯

D Allows the manufacturer to find out how well it is selling. ◯

3 Which of the following information can manufacturers choose to put on a label. Tick the correct options.

A A detailed description ◯   **B** Serving suggestions ◯

C A bar code ◯   **D** Best before date or sell by date ◯

E Environmental issues ◯   **F** Special claims ◯

Environmental Symbols

4 The table contains some of the environmental symbols found on labels. Match the descriptions **A, B, C** with the symbols **1, 2, 3**. Enter the appropriate number in the boxes provided.

A Do not litter ◯

B Glass can be recycled and should be put in a bottle bank ◯

C Mobius loop ◯

	Symbol
1	
2	
3	

Packaging

Functions of Packaging

1 The following are functions of packaging. Match the description **A, B, C** with the level of packaging **1, 2, 3**. Enter the appropriate number in the boxes provided.

A Contains the food product ◯

B Holds several products together ◯

C Used when products are being transported to the point of sale ◯

	Level of Packaging
1	Secondary
2	Transit
3	Primary

2 Choose the correct words from the options given to complete the following sentences.

advertise　　　**transportation**　　　**extends**　　　**tampering**　　　**physical**

a) Primary packaging preserves and _____ shelf life.

b) Transit packaging contains food during _____.

c) Packaging is used to _____ and inform.

d) Packaging protects food from _____ damage.

e) Packaging is used to prevent _____.

Card and Paperboard

3 Which of the following are advantages of card and paperboard? Tick the correct options.

A They are easily printed on ◯

B They are cheap ◯

C They are waterproof ◯

D They can be produced in different thicknesses ◯

Glass

4 Fill in the missing words to complete the following sentences.

The advantages of using glass are that it's _____ so consumers can see the product.

It's _____ resistant, rigid and can be _____. The disadvantages

are that it's _____, heavy and expensive to _____.

◯

Packaging

Metal

1 Which of the following isn't an advantage of using metal? Tick the correct option.

    A It can be easy to open ◯   **B** It is recyclable ◯

    C It is easy to print on ◯   **D** It extends shelf life ◯

2 Give one disadvantage of using metal.

_____

_____

Plastics

3 Circle the correct options in the following sentences.

    a) Different types of plastic have **the same / individual** characteristics.

    b) **Some / All** plastics are recyclable.

    c) One **advantage / disadvantage** of using plastic is that it is lightweight.

    d) Plastic is **expensive / cheap** to produce.

    e) It is **easy / difficult** to print on plastic.

4 Which of the following are advantages of using plastic? Tick the correct options.

    A Some are heat resistant ◯   **B** Plastic is resistant to acids ◯

    C Plastic is heavy ◯   **D** It can be flexible or rigid ◯

    E All plastics are biodegradable ◯   **F** Plastic is durable ◯

Plastics Used for Packaging

5 Four main plastics are used in packaging. Which one is described below?

It has good heat insulation, can be brittle and is used for clam shells for take away food. Tick the correct option.

    A PP ◯

    B PET ◯

    C PVC ◯

    D PS ◯

Exam Style Questions

1 a) A person who is unable to eat wheat products is a:

    i) Vegan ◯   ii) Coeliac ◯

    iii) Diabetic ◯   iv) Vegetarian ◯

b) Which piece of equipment doesn't use CAM?

    i) Electronic scales ◯   ii) Bread maker ◯

    iii) Blender ◯   iv) Grater ◯

c) Braising is a wet method of cooking. Which is another wet method?

    i) Grilling ◯   ii) Barbecuing ◯

    iii) Poaching ◯   iv) Roasting ◯

d) Citrus fruit is a good source of:

    i) Iron ◯   ii) Vitamin C ◯

    iii) Calcium ◯   iv) Vitamin D ◯

e) Which isn't a finishing technique?

    i) Kneading ◯   ii) Glazing ◯

    iii) Icing ◯   iv) Piping ◯

f) The number of fruit and vegetable portions you should eat each day is:

    i) 6   ii) 8   iii) 4   iv) 5

g) What is the pH range of acids:

    i) pH 8–14   ii) pH 1–6   iii) pH 5–7   iv) pH 6–14

h) Which of the following isn't a layered product?:

    i) Tiramisu   ii) Lasagne   iii) Trifle   iv) Chow Mein

(8 x 1 mark)

i) Which of the following could you buy at a local farmers market?

   i) Grapes ◯   ii) Pomegranate ◯

   iii) Apples ◯   iv) Pineapple ◯

j) Which of the following packaging is not biodegradable?

   i) Paperboard ◯   ii) Glass ◯

   iii) Aluminium ◯

k) The effect of adding an anti-caking agent to a food is to?

   i)   measure volume ◯

   ii) improve nutritional value ◯

   iii) improve texture ◯

   iv) prevent dry ingredients "clumping" (sticking together) ◯

l) In which milk process is milk treated to 72°C for 15 seconds?

   i) UHT ◯   ii) Pasteurisation ◯

   iii) Sterilisation ◯   iv) Canning ◯

m) The addition of nutrients to food is called:

   i) Flavour enhancing ◯   ii) Nourishment ◯

   iii) Fortification ◯   iv) Dietary requirements ◯

n) Which of the following wouldn't a vegan eat?

   i) Jam   ii) Marmalade   iii) Honey   iv) Marmite

o) Where in the home would you store fresh dairy products?

   i) Freezer   ii) Cupboard   iii) Fridge   iv) Larder

(7 x 1 mark)

Total = 15 marks

Exam Style Questions

1 **Healthy Weight, Healthy Lives** is a government strategy aimed at lowering obesity and excess weight. Explain what food manufacturers have done to support this strategy.

....

....

....

....

....

....

....

....

....

....

....

....

.... *(6 marks)*

2 a) A test kitchen is developing design ideas for a savoury snack. The savoury snack will be sold at supermarkets. The snack product must meet the following design criteria:

- Use a bread base.
- Have a savoury filling or topping.
- Contain organic vegetables.
- Be able to be eaten hot or cold.
- Be a single portion.

Question two continues overleaf

Design two different products that may be developed. Use notes and sketches to show your ideas. No packaging ideas should be included.

Design Idea A	Name of Product

(5 marks)

Design Idea B	Name of Product

(5 marks)

2 b) Which idea would you choose?

.... (*no marks*)

2 c) Explain how your chosen design meets the design criteria.

Criteria	How is it met
Use a bread base	
Have a savoury filling /topping	
Contain organic vegetables	
Be able to be eaten hot or cold	

(*4 marks*)

2 d) What processes and control checks would be needed to make your chosen product in a test kitchen. You can use flow charts, notes, annotation and sketches to show these.

(10 marks)

2 e) The following ingredients are used by a manufacturer in making a pizza base.

Explain why each ingredient is used, giving a different reason for each one.

Ingredient for Pizza Base	Reason for use
Strong plain flour	
Sugar	
Salt	
Yeast	
Water	

(5 marks)

3 a) What type of flour would be used to make an apple pie?

(1 mark)

Exam Style Questions

3 b) Explain how to make shortcrust pastry using the rubbing-in method.

....

....

....

.... *(3 marks)*

3 c) Using notes and sketches describe two different methods of giving a quality finish to an apple pie. Explain, giving different reasons, why you have chosen each finish.

Finish 1	Finish 2
(2 marks)	*(2 marks)*
Reasons for choice	**Reasons for choice**
(1 mark)	*(1 mark)*

Total = *(6 marks)*

© Lonsdale

85

Exam Style Questions

4 a) Manufacturers need to find out what consumers think about existing products when designing new products. Give three examples of research methods used.

i) ....

ii) ....

iii) ....

(3 x 1 mark = 3 marks)

4 b) Disassembly is used by the designer to develop their ideas. Give four things that could be found out by disassembling a lemon meringue pie.

i) ....

ii) ....

iii) ....

iv) ....

(4 x 1 mark = 4 marks)

4 c) Designers model ideas using the computer. Explain four reasons why this is used.

i) ....

....

ii) ....

....

iii) ....

....

iv) ....

....

(4 x 1 mark = 4 marks)

5 a) A test kitchen is trialling a new pasta salad. State four reasons why this is done.

i) ....

....

ii) ....

....

iii) ....

....

iv) ....

....

(4 x 1 mark = 4 marks)

5 b) Controlled conditions ensure reliable results in sensory analysis. Explain what these conditions are and explain the reasons why they are required.

....

....

....

....

....

....

....

....

....

(5 marks)

5 c) The ingredients are shown below for a new pasta salad being trialled in a test.

200g pasta shells cooked   50g diced cucumber
for 8 minutes   50g diced green pepper
½ tsp mango chutney   1 stick celery diced
½ tsp curry powder   20g diced onion
4 tbsp mayonnaise   20g raisins
1 tsp tomato sauce

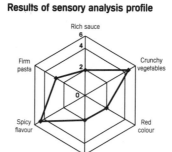

Results of sensory analysis profile

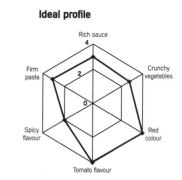

Ideal profile

Explain the changes that could be made to make the pasta salad match the ideal profile more closely.

Area for Improvement	Adaptations
Tomato flavour	
Spicy flavour	
Red colour of sauce	
Firmness of pasta	

(4 x1 mark)

6 a) The table below shows tools and equipment. Complete the table below by giving missing names and uses.

Equipment	Name	Use

(8 marks)

b) What safety precautions would be needed when using electrical equipment in the test kitchen?

(3 marks)

7 A pizza manufacturer uses the following standard components:

Pizza base
Passata (tomato sauce)
Grated mozzarella
Tinned tuna fish

7 a) Give four advantages of using standard components?

i) ....

ii) ....

iii) ....

iv) ....

(4 x 1 mark = 4 marks)

7 b) Give four disadvantages of using standard components?

i) ....

ii) ....

iii) ....

iv) ....

(4 x 1 mark = 4 marks)

8 a) Give the names of two food poisoning bacteria.

i) ....

ii) ....

(2 x 1 mark = 2 marks)

8 b) List four symptoms of food poisoning.

i) ....

ii) ....

iii) ....

iv) ....

(4 x 1 mark = 4 marks)

8 c) 'High risk foods are most likely to cause food poisoning'. Explain this statement.

....

....

....

....

....

....

....

....

....

....

....

....

(6 marks)

8 d) Explain how to use a food probe correctly on a cooked chicken.

(4 marks)

8 e) Colour coded equipment is used when preparing foods. Why is this necessary?

(6 marks)

8 f) Food handlers must wear protective clothing. Fill in the chart to give details of the type of clothing.

	Type of Protective Clothing
Head and face	.... (*2 marks*)
Hand and arms	.... (*2 marks*)
Feet	.... (*2 marks*)
Body	.... (*2 marks*)

8 g) In addition to wearing protective clothing, give four other rules that food handlers must follow to ensure that food is handled hygienically.

i) ....

ii) ....

iii) ....

iv) ....

(*4 x 1 mark = 4 marks*)

Exam Style Questions

9 a) Manufacturers use different production methods. State two advantages of batch production.

    i) ....

    ii) ....

(2 x 1 mark = 2 marks)

9 b) State two advantages of continuous flow production.

    i) ....

    ii) ....

(2 x 1 mark = 2 marks)

9 c) State two advantages of one-off production (jobbing).

    i) ....

    ii) ....

(2 x 1 mark = 2 marks)

9 d) Sensors are used in manufacturing processes. Fill in the chart to show the use of each of the following sensors.

Sensor	Use
Weight load	
Temperature sensor	
pH level sensor	
Electronic eye	
Metal detector	

(5 x 1 mark = 5 marks)

10 a) The following information was found on the labelling of a fresh fruit cream trifle. How do these labels inform the consumer?

   i) Use by: ....

         ....

         ....

   ii) Best before: ....

         ....

         ....

         ....

   iii) Display until: ....

   iv)   ....

         ....

   v) May contain nuts: ....

         ....

         ....

(5 x 1 mark = 5 marks)

10 b) How are the ingredients in products listed in the label?

....

....

(2 marks)

10 c) Who is responsible for checking that labels are accurate and not misleading?

....

(1 mark)

Exam Style Questions

11 Explain why food is packaged. Give examples in your answer.

_____

_____

_____

_____

_____

(4 marks)

12 a) Explain what is meant by 'food miles'.

_____

_____

(2 marks)

12 b) Why should food miles be reduced?

_____

_____

(2 marks)

12 c) How can food miles be reduced?

_____

_____

(2 marks)

12 d) Packaging has an impact on the environment. Explain how this impact can be reduced.

_____

_____

_____

(3 marks)